Raising Awesome Kids

Reloaded

Other Books by Sam and Geri Laing

Friends and Lovers:
Marriage As God Designed It
(Sam and Geri Laing)

The Wonder Years:
Parenting Teens and Preteens
(Sam and Geri Laing, Elizabeth Laing Thompson)

Be Still My Soul:
A Practical Guide to a Deeper Relationship with God
(Sam Laing)

The Guilty Soul's Guide to Grace:
Opening the Door to Freedom in Christ
(Sam Laing)

Mighty Man of God:
A Return to the Glory of Manhood
(Sam Laing)

A Life Worth Living:
Focusing on What Really Matters
(Geri Laing)

The Five Senses of Romantic Love:
God's Plan for Exciting Sexual Intimacy in Marriage
(Sam Laing)

Raising Awesome Kids Reloaded

Being the Most Important Influence
in Your Children's Lives

Sam and Geri Laing

DPI
DISCIPLESHIP
PUBLICATIONS
INTERNATIONAL

www.dpibooks.org

To John Oliver Laing, Sr., and Agnes Laing
and to Frank A. Guba and Jane Guba,

our beloved parents,

*For all of your untold sacrifices,
for all you have given,
we give you our thanks and
our undying love.*

Contents

Foreword 8

Original Introduction...10

Introduction Reloaded 14

PART ONE: FOUNDATIONS

Chapter 1   First Things First 19

Chapter 2   Husband and Father 27

Chapter 3   Wife and Mother.............................49

Chapter 4   New Mothers....................................74

PART TWO: FUNDAMENTALS

Chapter 5   The Four Essentials 93

Chapter 6   Winning Obedience from Children.................110

Chapter 7   God's Training Plan 129

Chapter 8   Nurturing Confidence in Children 138

PART THREE: FABRIC

Chapter 9   Foundations of a Spiritual Family 155

Chapter 10   A Close Family 169

Chapter 11   Anxious Parents.............................183

Chapter 12   Heart-to-Heart Talks 198

PART FOUR: FINISHING

Chapter 13   A Torrent of Technology 211

Chapter 14   Sex and Dating 224

Chapter 15   Special Life Situations...................242

Chapter 16   Conversion 254

Epilogue 266

Recommended Reading 269

Foreword

Fourteen years, $120,000 in college tuition, one wedding, five moves, two dogs, three years of infertility followed by three babies (in three years!)...a lot has happened since I wrote the foreword to my parents' first book—and that's just *my* life, let alone the rest of the Laing clan!

It has been such an adventure watching our family mature and our adult lives begin to unfold. I must confess that, in the aftermath of the book's original publication, my siblings and I occasionally grew tired of the ill-suited "Brady Bunch" references and the continual "awesome kid" barbs—but we have never lost our appreciation for the remarkable parents and family that we have.

I have felt so proud watching my brother David enter the ministry, marry and begin to raise his son; seeing Jonathan earn his MBA and begin pursuing a business career while still serving God wholeheartedly; and watching Alexandra shine as a student leader in her campus ministry.

It gives me such hope that, if I imitate the lifestyle and patterns I saw growing up, my own children may one day give me the same cause for pride and joy. To this day, we enjoy being together as a family more than anything...and I always pray that my husband, Kevin, and I can build the same closeness in our own family.

The ten years that I have spent serving in campus ministries across the Southeast have reinforced my convictions that family makes an indelible difference in the people we become. Time and again, I have counseled young women as they have wrestled with the consequences of their upbringing. And while a godly family does not guarantee a perfect life or a responsible kid, it sure does help—giving people the foundation for righteousness and character, the basis upon which to make wise life decisions.

My parents' parenting has never really stopped—although it is certainly different now than it once was. When I married, they stepped aside and allowed Kevin to take the primary role of spiritual influence in my life, but they have never failed to give advice and encouragement when I have needed it...as I often do. As I have begun to raise my own children—we are still waiting for the mild-mannered, easygoing child that I fear does not exist in our shared gene pool—my appreciation for my upbringing has grown even more. My mother is still my greatest guide as I try to hang on to my sanity and somehow instill a love for God into three stubborn toddler hearts.

I recently spoke to a friend who lamented her feelings of inadequacy and insecurity as she raises her young children. After growing up in an unstable home marred by drug addiction and deceit, she is striving to build a Christian family of her own. She feels keenly the void in her past—she has no helpful experiences to draw upon.

Her regrets have made me even more grateful that I have such powerful, personal memories to call upon in my own moments of parenting need. Although I am no parenting expert, at the very least I have a godly pattern and a wealth of family experiences filed away in my heart, so that when my two-year-old stares up at me, her beautiful black eyes radiating a defiance so intense it makes my head spin—I do not feel completely lost...just semi-completely lost!

I say this to encourage every parent to keep fighting to lead your family in a godly way. Your children, whether you know it or not—and whether they admit it or not—are watching and absorbing all that you do, and your family will reap the benefits of your efforts for generations to come. It is my heartfelt hope and prayer that one day—even through these times that seem to grow ever more troubled—*all* of us who read this book can thank God for graciously enabling us to raise "awesome kids" of our own!

Elizabeth Laing Thompson

Original Introduction

"I'm out here, Daddy...I'm out here, Daddy...I'm out here, Daddy..." My daughter, repeating her words in a rhythmic monotone as only a two-year-old can, seemed to go on and on, insistent but polite in her determination to be heard. She stood in the kitchen and spoke through the closed door into the dining room where I was seated at the table working.

It was Saturday night, and the hour was drawing late. I still had no idea for the sermon I was to preach the next morning. Anxiety and frustration mounted within me, only further stifling the ability to think perceptively and creatively. The voice of young Elizabeth, who had just had her bath and was all set for bed, only made matters worse. She just wanted to say good night, but I was preoccupied.

"Not now, honey; Daddy's busy." But she would not be turned away.

"I'm out here, Daddy," came back the reply.

I repeated my rebuff a few more times, as pleasantly as I could, but to no avail.

"I'm out here, Daddy...I'm out here, Daddy."

I tried the silent treatment. Maybe if I did not say anything, she would get tired and go away.

But after a few moments, the little voice spoke again, "I'm out here, Daddy."

I finally realized this was getting nowhere and that I would have to let her in. "Okay, honey, come on in, but Daddy is really busy."

The self-closing swinging door that separated the dining room from the kitchen creaked slowly open, then closed with the ka whoom-whoom-whoom sound it always made as it settled back into its normal position. I kept my eyes glued to my work, hoping that Elizabeth would now be satisfied. She silently entered and stood a few feet behind my chair. I continued to work, straining for a sermon topic, but nothing would come to mind. My concentration was so intense that I completely forgot that my young daughter was still in the room.

Then I heard, from directly behind my chair, the soft, small voice of Elizabeth saying, "I'm in here, Daddy."

I'm in here, Daddy. Isn't that what our children are trying to tell us? They are "in here" with us, and they need us. The world is "out there," and it is troubling and hard and seemingly getting more difficult to cope with every passing year. We simply must take the few precious years we have with our children and make the most of the time.

This is a book to help you to be a better parent. In it, Geri and I share with you some of what we have gleaned from the Scriptures and what we have learned from the wonderful experience of raising our four children. We hope these lessons will help you as much as they have helped us.

We do not presume to be perfect parents or to have a perfect family. But we are trying to do it God's way, and he has blessed us amazingly. We love the life God has given us, and our family is having a blast living it together!

Let me assure you that our children have given us their permission to tell you all the different stories that involve them. We do not wish to embarrass our kids, nor do we long for them to be put on a pedestal. They, like their mom and dad, are only human, with their strengths and weaknesses. If sharing some of the specifics about our household and its members can help you, then the Laing family is happy for you to know us as we really are.

Please, study this book carefully before you try to implement everything in it. More than a "how to" manual, it is intended to be a means to help you think and act with godly attitudes. So many things we discuss in these pages are difficult to present with the proper weight, emphasis and clarity and can be easily misunderstood and misapplied. We especially want you to grasp that the strong discipline and high standards that we urge in child rearing must be carried out in an atmosphere of love, joy and happiness.

If you and your family need additional help and advice, we encourage you to seek the counsel of mature, spiritual disciples and experienced church leaders. The situations some of you face may require wise, objective help, perhaps over a period of time.

But we never finished our story! Elizabeth was left standing forlornly behind my chair, wasn't she?

After hearing her words, I put down my pen, turned to her, smiled and took her into my arms. Warm tears of affection welled up freely in my eyes. I held her and talked with her for a few minutes, hugged her again and put her down. She toddled back to her room smiling and contented, ready to be put to bed.

I do not remember what I preached the next morning, and I'm sure no one else does either. But as long as I live, I will never forget the lesson God taught me that Saturday night so many years ago.

My daughter was trying to tell me something, and at first, I was not listening. She needed my love and attention and did not know how to say it. She wanted to be with me, but I was "too busy."

As Elizabeth grew through her teen and college years, she would often come quietly into the room where I was and just sit down. After a few moments of silence I would ask, "Honey, would you like to talk for a minute?" and we did. We would hug at the end, and she would walk away contented and smiling. Every time I watched her leave, I was thankful I finally got the message that night when she was only two years old.

May you hear the voices of your children, whether they speak aloud or reach out to you silently with longing in their eyes. They are with you for only a few precious years. Sooner than you realize, they will be "out there" in a world that can devour them if you have not raised them well. Give them all you can while they are "in here" with you in your home. They will turn out awesome!

And if we, by the efforts we have made in this volume, can help you to do a better job of that, then we have not written in vain.

Sam and Geri Laing, 1994

Introduction
Reloaded

Life has changed dramatically since the first edition of *Raising Awesome Kids* came out in 1994. Cell phones, iPods, Facebook, Y2K, 9/11, an economy spiraling downward...all of these changes can leave parents feeling that they are falling even further behind in doing what is already just about the hardest job on the planet.

Times change, but the principles of God's word do not. As parents we need to be aware of what is going on around us, but continually return to the eternal wisdom of Scripture where alone is found the infallible wisdom we so desperately need.

Geri and I have not only updated the information throughout the already existing chapters, but we have also added three new chapters to address the technological advances that can bewilder us, the pressures of a society whose pace of life is increasing and whose morals are decreasing, and the ever-present need of parents to connect on a heart level with their kids.

The original *Raising Awesome Kids* helped a whole generation of Christian parents raise their kids. It is our prayer that this new and updated version will do the same for the moms and dads of the new millennium.

When we wrote the original volume, our children were ages seventeen, fourteen, twelve and six. Now, they are thirty-two, twenty-nine, twenty-six and twenty. Our two oldest, Elizabeth and David, are both married, and are parents. Jonathan has earned his Master's degree and is working in another state, and Alexandra is in her junior year of college. Where did the time go? It only seems like yesterday that the six of us were having family meals together and going on vacations in our minivan.

As much as we look back with joy on those wonderful years, we are deeply happy with where our family is now. All of our children are devoted Christians, and they remain close to us and to each other. The two who are married have wonderful spouses, and the grandkids are just amazing. Had you asked me as a young man if my life could have turned out any better, I would have not been able to imagine the blessings God has poured out upon me.

The biblical principles we wrote about in the original book worked. When we wrote in 1994, we were in the midst of trying to raise our kids the way we thought God wanted us to, as best we could determine from the Scriptures. Anything right that we did came from God. Any good results are to his glory and are the gifts of his grace and the product of his wisdom. Left to our own devices, we would not have known what to do, and we would have lost our way.

God knows how to do things right. His word is his loving gift to guide us, not just in how to get to heaven, but in how to live. If we take it into our heart and mind, and put it into our real life, we are blessed beyond imagination.

We didn't do everything perfectly. Not then, and not now. There are some things we would do better and differently if we could do them over. Our family was not a perfect one, unusually prearranged by God to be harmonious, happy and peaceful. We struggled with our sins, our weaknesses, our failures, our shortcomings and our inadequacies just like everyone else does. There were some dark days—no, some dark weeks, months and even a few darker years.

But through all those years, God's grace and love were with us. His mercy pardoned our offenses, his love covered our sins, and his Spirit guided and empowered us when we lost our way and ran out of strength.

And, he is still with us now. There is more to do. We have two kids yet to marry off. And, in spite of our wishing it were different, we can't arrange their marriages for them! We have grandkids to enjoy—and to help along the way to heaven. We have more work for God left to do. We have more books to write, more sermons to preach, more lessons to give, more people to help. And, we have more sermons to hear and more lessons to learn.

Each day of my life I thank God for the blessing of every moment he has given me with my wife and my children, and now, with my son-in-law and daughter-in-law, and my grandchildren. Next to going to heaven, there is no greater joy in my life.

I know, and Geri knows, from Whom these blessings flow. They come from the One who ran out to meet us when we came to our senses and headed home, back to our Father's house. He hugged us, kissed us, interrupted our confession with the bestowal of his pardon, love, acceptance and dignity. He gave us his best and threw us a party. And since then, the celebration has never really stopped. The music and dancing continue, and one day, in our permanent home, they will go on unabated and undimmed, where sorrows are forgot, and love's true joys are fully restored.

Sam and Geri Laing
Athens, Georgia
October 2008

Part 1
Foundations

Chapter 1

First Things First

Unless the LORD builds the house,
its builders labor in vain.
Psalm 127:1

Most of us have someone or something that we love most in this world. Who or what is it for you? Think now, and be honest. If you need help, ask your children to answer the question for you. If they are old enough, they will know, and they will tell you the unadorned truth. Upon the answer to this question hinge all of your hopes, your dreams and your capacities to raise your children to a joyful end. If the answer is what it should be, then the rest of this book can be a powerful tool to help you. But if the answer is wrong, then you are doomed to frustration, heartache and failure. No amount of counsel, however wise, can repair your house, if the Lord is not the builder.

Jesus must be our first love. He must be our life's greatest passion. He must *be* our life, not just a part of it. He will not be added in as one more calendar item to round out our personal or family life. He must be the hub of the wheel, not one of many spokes. He will not be the copilot. He is either the pilot, or he is out of the plane.

Jesus expected people to be disciples:

"And anyone who does not carry his cross and follow me cannot be my disciple." (Luke 14:27)

He elaborated with these words:

"If anyone would come after me, he must deny himself and take up his cross and follow me. For whoever wants to save his life will lose it, but whoever loses his life for me and for the gospel will save it. What good is it for a man to gain the whole world, yet forfeit his soul?" (Mark 8:34–36)

Paul said it this way:

When Christ, who is your life, appears, then you also will appear with him in glory. (Colossians 3:4)

I have been crucified with Christ and I no longer live, but Christ lives in me. (Galatians 2:20)

For to me, to live is Christ, and to die is gain.
(Philippians 1:21)

We must put first things first. This is the key to everything, not just the impractical theory we discard before getting to the "real thing" of how to raise kids.

Merely being religious will not do the job. Even deep involvement in a fired-up church is not enough. Your kids must see that Jesus is a real person to you and that you walk with him and love him as a brother. Your faith must make a real difference in the person you are at home, because that is who you really are. There is no acting at home, just real life. Kids can spot insincerity or external devotion a mile away, and they will be turned off or even embittered if they perceive us as less than genuine.

Having said this, let us hasten to add that there is no absolute guarantee given in Scripture that if parents are deeply committed Christians, their kids will follow suit. There are devoted Christians whose children have not become disciples, or who made the decision to follow Christ, only to abandon it later. God has given all of us, including the children of godly people, a free will. And, sometimes, in spite of our best efforts, children may exercise that will to turn away from Jesus.

What we are saying is that if there are major issues in the discipleship of parents, if there are large areas of life not under the Lordship of Christ, then the chances of our children coming to Jesus may be seriously impaired.

All parents struggle, and none of us is perfect. Our children know our weaknesses, and will forgive us for them. But hypocrisy in our lives can kill the faith and idealism of our children.

Or, there may be another problem. It may be that while we follow the teachings of Jesus in most areas of our own lives, we ignore, or are less than diligent on *how to impart* the teachings of Scripture to our kids. We do not carefully listen to God on *how to be good parents.*

In other words, some of us may be more influenced by the wisdom of man than of God in how to raise our kids. If we do not follow biblical teaching on what to expect of our kids, how to impart faith, how to help build a heart for God in them, how to teach and train them, how to love and discipline them, then the result may be a breakdown in the path of transmission. This can mean that while we ourselves will go to heaven, we may not effectively impart our convictions to our children.

Please know that we say these things not to discourage you or to be unkind, but to inspire, awaken and help you to be the very best parent you can be.

I want to share with you a birthday card my son Jonathan wrote for me when he was ten years old. I do this to let you see

21

how highly a child values our love for God, and how keenly they can perceive it, even from an early age.

10/7/98

> Dear Dad,
> Happy B-day!!!!!!!!! You made it! Ha! Ha! Ha! Ha!! I love you so very much!!!! My arm would fall off if I tryed list all the things you do for me! You are the best dad, on this Earth!! You are so disipline, you have quiet-times every day but most of all you have such an awesome heart for God!!! I really admire that alot. You have taught me so much. Like football, I use to not even be able to throw one! With-out you I would be a wimpy little kid!! ☺ I hope you've had an awesome birthday and like your new things!! I love you alot! Goodnight!!!!!!!!!!!!!
>
> Love,
> Jonathan Laing
> JONATHAN LAING

There are many things in Jonathan's card that touched me, but that which moved and surprised me the most was his feelings and observations about my closeness to God. I never thought, at the age of ten, that he noticed such things. But

22

notice he did, and it moved him. The battle for his soul was more than half won already! And, it is something he carries with him to this day. The cards he now writes me have the same sentiments as the one he wrote when he was ten.

Some of us made the decision to make Jesus Lord in the past, but where are we today? We were at one time zealous and devoted—perhaps before we got married or had children. Since that time, various life changes may have distracted us. As Geri often says, "The longer I live, the more I see how hard it is to make it all the way, faithful to the end."

It is so easy to allow "life's worries, riches and pleasures" and "the deceitfulness of wealth, and the desires for other things" to come in and choke out our relationship with God (Luke 8:14, Mark 4:19). The gifts God has given us—our spouses, our children, our jobs—can become paramount and displace our love for the Giver. Or, we can allow even legitimate concerns to so worry and distract us that our minds are no longer spiritually focused.

If this is your condition, seek the Lord again with all your heart. Put him back in the place of supremacy. If God is first, you have the foundation upon which to build an awesome family.

Assuming God is first, who's next on our list? Who gets the nod for second place? *Next in line to God comes our husband or wife.* They must be that special person that we love more than anyone else on earth. More than our love for our mother or father, more than our love for our children, or anyone or anything else, our devotion to our lifetime companion must be the greatest earthly love of all.

Our spouse is the one person to whom we are physically and spiritually united until death. Listen to the words of Jesus:

> "Haven't you read," he replied, "that at the beginning the Creator 'made them male and female,' and said 'For this reason a man will leave his father and mother and be united to his wife, and the two will become one flesh'? So they

> are no longer two but one. Therefore what God has joined
> together, let man not separate." (Matthew 19:4-6)

One day (hopefully!) our offspring will grow up and leave home. We raise our children to go out and build their own lives, but we stay with our marriage partner for life. The kids are our flesh and blood, but we are "one flesh" with our spouse. The difference is absolutely critical.

Some of us have poured all our love into our children, and in so doing have neglected our marriages.

This reversal of priorities, while intended to help our kids, will ultimately damage them. They are not meant to be in that special position. God reserves this place for the husband or wife alone. If your world revolves around your children, it makes them arrogant, insecure or both. Kids do not find their true joy and confidence from being put on a pedestal; they find it first from God, then from their mom and dad being deeply in love.

It is so easy for a marriage to grow cold, for the exciting, romantic love to fade away. We find ourselves saying things like, "We're so busy, and we have kids now, and we just don't have time for each other like we used to." Know this: *next to loving God first, there is no other more important thing you will ever do for your children than to be deeply and intimately in love with your spouse.*

Take an honest look at your marriage. Have you drifted apart? Is there emptiness where there once was a fullness of joy? Is there constant bickering and arguing? A tense, cold atmosphere? An ongoing war for supremacy? Cutting, sarcastic, harsh remarks? Raised voices? Arguments in front of or within earshot of the kids? If so, we appeal to you, for your sake and for your children's sake, take action and get help.

Sometimes we think the children are unaware, and that our marriage problems have little effect on them. No, those little eyes see more than we realize, and those little ears are fine-tuned

24

to our frequency. They can sense when things aren't right between Mom and Dad, and it troubles them. Kids hate it when their parents bicker and quarrel. They long for us to love each other, to laugh together and to be close.

Why is it that when Mom and Dad hug, the kids want to nuzzle in between, and start giggling and teasing? It is because they love it when we love each other. It gives them a sense of peace, happiness and security and lets them know that all is well and that the family is going to stay together.

Much of the anger and rebellion in kids today can be traced back to problem marriages. Children living in fear and tension cannot relax and enjoy life. They worry their hearts out. They try to fix everything. They choose sides. They end up resenting their parents, disliking themselves and possibly even blaming themselves.[1]

Geri and I decided that even after we had kids, we would focus on keeping our marriage close. We even made it our goal to maintain a good romantic life (just for the sake of the kids, of course!).

I'll never forget an incident that so clearly affirmed this lesson. It happened when our son David was about three. We were in the car, and David and a playmate were in the back seat. Geri and I leaned over and gave each other a little kiss. David's pal immediately yelled out, "Ewwwww! Your mom and dad kissed! My mom and dad *never* kiss!" From his tone, you would have thought we had been caught shoplifting or something.

David looked at his friend quizzically. Then he turned to him, leaned over, and said proudly: "Well, my mom and dad kiss *a lot!*"

---

1. Some of you reading this book are doing all you can to have a good marriage, but it may be that your spouse is not a committed Christian or perhaps not as devoted to your marriage and family as they should be. In such cases you must do all you can as an individual to set the example and provide the guidance that your children need, trusting God to make up for whatever else may be lacking. There are many instances in the Scriptures and in our own experience that show that wonderful kids can be raised in less than ideal circumstances.

Here then, is the first and most important lesson in this book: *to love God first, and to deeply and happily love one another, is the greatest gift you can ever give your children.* In our case, it took hard work, prayer, many apologies (mostly from me!) and lots of determination and patience. God honored those resolves and gave plenty of grace for our shortcomings—and so he will for you as well.

It may seem that the challenges in your family loom up to heaven, but if you seek to build your family God's way, know that your efforts are not in vain. The things you are teaching your kids will remain with them, even if sometimes it seems they aren't getting it. Learn, grow and persist. And, one day, even long after your children are grown, they will remember that you taught them the most important lessons they ever learned, and they will be thankful.

Husband and Father

> Husbands, love your wives, just as Christ loved the church and gave himself up for her.... Fathers, do not exasperate your children; instead, bring them up in the training and instruction of the Lord.
>
> Ephesians 5:25, 6:4

My last memory of my father forever will be with me. He was lying upon his bed in our home, emaciated by cancer, knowing the end was near. I was twelve years old, the youngest of five children. He called us all in, spoke his last words, and we saw him for the final time. I do not remember what he said. I only remember the love I felt and the gift he gave me. He wanted me to have his beautiful twenty-gauge shotgun, the one he used for quail hunting. I remember the embrace, the tears and his heart for me. I treasure the gift he gave me and the memories it evokes of the wonderful times we spent together hunting in the North Florida fields where I grew up.

I have thought back through my childhood many times. I have sought to recall every positive, joyful memory of my dad and our relationship. There are many, and they move me to tears even as I write these words.

The sad thing is that my dad and I did not connect that deeply during those brief twelve years we had together. It was not that he did not try or that he did not care; some things just got in the way. My father had a temper and would sometimes raise his voice, not necessarily at me, but perhaps at someone else or at something that frustrated him. Now that I am older and I have to confront my own temper, I have much more understanding and compassion for him. But at the time, as a child, I withdrew in fear, hurt, rebellion and anger.

It was years later, after viewing the film *Field of Dreams*, that I saw my problem. The movie told the story of a rebellious son's vision of his dad when his father was still a young man, "before life had broken him down." It moved me so deeply (as it did many men) that afterwards I could scarcely speak. It sparked in me a deeper love for my father and enabled me to face and excise the root of bitterness that had so long grown within my heart. The burden of years of hurt and alienation disappeared, leaving behind only the wish that I, too, could have another chance to see my dad and to be as close as we both had longed to be.

I have since vowed that whatever I did, I would be close to my children. I promised God with all my heart to express to them my love, to be approachable, and to never allow any of them to be distant from me. God has blessed that commitment in a wonderful way. One of the incomparable rewards of my life is the closeness I enjoy with all four of my children, and I know they all feel the same way.

Our relationship with our father is, in many ways, the defining relationship in all of our lives. From it we develop our fundamental view of God and of ourselves. From this most basic of bonds also comes our response to authority and our self-confidence. This is why God places the responsibility of training children squarely upon the father: "Fathers...bring them up in the training and instruction of the Lord" (Ephesians 6:4).

This is not to diminish the mother's responsibility, but to give the proper emphasis to the father's role, a role so grievously neglected and misconceived in today's world. I believe that the increasing violence, chaos and emotional disturbance in many teenagers is a direct result of the absent or failing fathers in our homes.

Paul described the responsibilities of a husband and father in Ephesians 5:22–6:4, one of the definitive passages on the subject. His instructions can be summarized by two things: to *lead* and to *love*. We will examine them both.

Part 1

The Father As Leader

"For the husband is the head of the wife as Christ is the head of the church" (Ephesians 5:23) and as such is the head of the entire family. This means that you, as a father, are in charge. Under God, this responsibility is yours. It is neither arrogant nor presumptuous for you to lead. It is wrong *not* to lead.

The marriage is a partnership, to be sure, but the husband is the senior partner. The family functions as a group, but it is not a democracy. It has a leader who will listen, weigh and consider, but who has the charge, challenge and accountability for the final decision.

Men and women are of equal worth in the eyes of God (Galatians 3:26–28), but in marriage and in the home they have different roles:

> Wives, submit to your husbands as to the Lord. For the husband is the head of the wife as Christ is the head of the church, his body, of which he is the Savior. Now as the church submits to Christ, so also wives should submit to their husbands in everything. (Ephesians 5:22–24)

That men are to lead is not merely social convention. It is intrinsic to the very nature of creation:

> Now I want you to realize that the head of every man is Christ, and the head of the woman is man, and the head of Christ is God. (1 Corinthians 11:31)

Whatever the full meaning of these passages may be, they make it clear that men are equipped and charged by God with the responsibility of leadership in the home.

As with all else in the Scriptures, we hurt ourselves and those close to us when we ignore or distort God's plan. Untold harm comes to families, to children, and indeed to whole cultures and nations when homes are not built on the principle of husband/father leadership. Even in the church we have been far too influenced by worldly and unbiblical thinking on this point. We will live to pay a price dearer than we can imagine unless we restore the role of male leadership in marriage and the family according to God's plan.

The place to start is in your own home. We will examine four different aspects of the father as leader.

1. Strength and Conviction

> "Then choose for yourselves this day whom you will serve.... But as for me and my household, we will serve the LORD." (Joshua 24:15)

Fathers, we should be the rock of our family who, with Joshua of old, says "My family will serve the Lord." We should be the one to hold high the standard of absolute commitment to Jesus, the church and righteous living. When the call goes forth in the kingdom of God for response and sacrifice, we must lead the way. Our personal walk with God and our zeal for saving the lost should be an inspiration. We must strive mightily to be the strongest and most spiritual disciple in the entire family. As head of his family, the church, Jesus is strong. And we should be, too.

The responsibility to initiate, plan and conduct family devotionals rests on our shoulders. It is also our job to make sure that the children are being discipled to Christ. We should also pray with and teach our wives and urge them forward in their walk with God.

If we have convictions, our family will be profoundly affected by them. If we are strong, our household will be all the stronger. As we lead, they follow. It is a natural thing for children to want to imitate the example of their father. They do it instinctively. But this is also true when fathers go astray. How many times have we seen the children of spiritually apathetic and indifferent fathers follow suit? Even if Mother or Grandmother is a saint, it may not be enough to turn the tide of a father's bad influence. As soon as they are old enough to go their own way, many of these kids quit the church. Boys, especially, may conclude that church is well and good for women and girls, or for little kids and old people, but not for them.

Men, we must not buy into the world's idea that being spiritual is a "woman thing." No! Look at the men of the Bible like Moses, Joshua, David, John the Baptist, Peter, Paul and Jesus. They were *men* in every sense of the word—in their masculinity, strength of character and courage. These are our true models of manhood.

As head of our families, it is requisite that we be strong *emotionally*. The challenges of life must not break us down into discouragement and despair. If we fall, who will stand? It is a sad thing to see the wife or children trying to be the emotional glue of the family because the father has been made into an ineffective leader by difficulties and pressures.

Life is hard. Strength is needed, not only for Christ's sake, but also for our families' sake: "For God did not give us a spirit of timidity, but a spirit of power, of love and of self discipline" (2 Timothy 1:7).

It is needful to be strong *physically*. Yes, you heard me right. A man should not be soft and effeminate. We do not have to be super-athletic, but we should not allow our bodies and health to deteriorate due to neglect and laziness. Peter describes the wife as "the weaker partner" (1 Peter 3:7), but I must say that some of us have made the "Big Fisherman" a liar. We are weaker than our wives spiritually, emotionally and physically. No wonder we get no respect!

Take care of yourself. Get out, and get some exercise. Take off some fat; put on some muscle. Tone up your physique. Detach yourself from the couch. Get moving. Play some sports. Break a sweat, for crying out loud!

Jesus was a carpenter. He walked everywhere he went. He was vigorous and active. Be like him. Your wife will admire you and be attracted to you. Your daughters will be proud for their girlfriends (and boyfriends!) to meet you. Your sons will love to spend time with you. There is something impressive about a man who stays in shape and retains a youthful energy and power as the years advance.[1]

An incident that brought this issue home to me happened when my daughter Elizabeth was three years old. There was a popular TV show (since reprised into multiple movies) about a wimpy guy who, upon provocation, transformed into a huge, unbelievably muscular, green behemoth called "The Incredible Hulk." While watching the show one night, Elizabeth turned to

---

1. Certainly those of you who face various physical challenges and limitations should not feel robbed of your manhood or of your ability to show your children a masculine example. You may not be able to do what others can do, but if you face whatever difficulty you have with courage, determination and faith, you will win the hearts and respect of your children. As Paul said in another context: "The gift is acceptable according to what one has, not according to what one does not have" (2 Corinthians 8:12). Whatever situation you are in, give your best. Do that and God will bless you and your children.

me and said, "Daddy, I love the Incredible Hulk. He's big and strong just like *you!*" After hearing that, I decided that this precocious child was blessed with insight and destined for greatness. I also decided that before she learned any better, I'd better renew my gym membership, get in shape and stay in shape!

2. Provision and Protection

> If anyone does not provide for his relatives, and especially for his immediate family, he has denied the faith and is worse than an unbeliever. (1 Timothy 5:8)

So Paul, tell us, how do you really feel about deadbeat dads?

Our families should never have to worry about where the next meal is coming from, if the lights and phone are going to be turned off, if the car is going to be repossessed, or if there will be a roof over their heads or clothes to wear. As men, we just don't want our families to ever be haunted by that kind of insecurity. They can know that as long as Dad is there, they have absolutely nothing to worry about. This is an issue not only of our commitment to God, but of our manhood. If our Heavenly Father provides for all our physical needs (Matthew 6:25–34), should we not imitate him in caring for our children?

Unless we are ill or disabled, we need to take full responsibility for the care of our families. We need to make our own way in the world. Stop living off your parents, the church, your friends and the government. Stop making your wife carry the financial load, working herself to death to keep the family from going under. Be a man. Get a job—one that pays a real salary and provides some benefits. Some men are dreamers and never "settle down and earn the bread they eat" (2 Thessalonians 3:12). Heed the wise words of Solomon: "He who works his land will have abundant food, but the one who chases fantasies will have his fill of poverty" (Proverbs 28:19).

Even when times are hard, we need to find something we can do to support our families. And if the job is not ideal, the Bible teaches us that "whatever you do, work at it with all your heart, as working for the Lord, not for men, since you know that you will receive an inheritance from the Lord as a reward. It is the Lord Christ you are serving" (Colossians 3:23-24). And, if we work hard, we will be rewarded by God: "Do you see a man skilled in his work? He will serve before kings; he will not serve before obscure men" (Proverbs 22:29).

Get adequate medical insurance. Make arrangements that if you should die or be incapacitated, your family will not become dependent. Be on top of your finances so that there is adequate cash flow and timely payment of bills. Start a savings account to provide a cash reserve for emergencies and larger purchases, and start planning now for your children's college education.

Take care of things around the house. If there is a yard, mow it. If there are leaves, rake them. If there is snow, shovel it. If there is furniture to be moved, get up off it and move it! Do the repair jobs and maintenance work. Change the filters, look after the car, paint the walls, take out the garbage. There are many frustrated wives out there who seemingly cannot get their husbands to lift a finger to help them. The kids will see this and will either disrespect us for our indolence or cheerfully imitate us in it. Happy is the family with a hard-working father! "If a man is lazy, the rafters sag; if his hands are idle, the house leaks" (Ecclesiastes 10:18).

But fathers are more than providers; we are also *protectors*. As protector we look out for and guard our families physically, emotionally and spiritually. We should watch out for our wives and children, making sure they are physically safe. There is no place for fretting and worry, but for calm, careful vigilance. If any family member is in a situation where they are being beaten down, crushed or completely overwhelmed, then it is time to act. We cannot and should not shield them from the realities of life, but we must protect them from any forces before which they are helpless.

3. Training and Teaching

Fathers...bring them up in the training and instruction of the Lord. (Ephesians 6:4)

We will devote a great deal of time in chapter 7 to the spiritual training of children. Here I speak of our role as a coach and a mentor—teaching kids the nuts-and-bolts skills of life. This is one of the most vital of our fatherly duties, and is one of the easiest to overlook and neglect.

Children love to learn and they love for their dads to teach them new things. In a special way, time spent teaching our children bonds us together. It says to a child that we love and value them when we give our time to patiently teach a skill. And, there is nothing that builds any more confidence in our kids than when they hear Dad say "Great job!"

What are we talking about? With younger children, it may be teaching a simple physical activity such as tying shoes. As they enter elementary school, we may need to teach them how to throw and catch, how to hit a baseball, or how to kick a soccer ball. My own father was quite a mechanic, and he taught me how to work with tools, change a spark plug, and run the lawn mower. Today, I still consider myself mechanically challenged, but I can at least hold my own with a screwdriver—and I shudder to think where I'd be without those early lessons. You are not going to be an expert in every area, but be assured—whatever you have to give is absolutely essential, and your kids will love you for it.

When your kids are in their preteen and teen years, Dad's help may be needed in teaching manners or in dating etiquette. When my son Jonathan went out on his first date, he was petrified.

"What are we supposed to talk about?" he asked. I came up with five questions for him to ask the young lady to get the conversation going.

When the big night arrived, he gathered his courage and sallied forth, emboldened by having committed Dad's questions to memory. I met him at the door when he came in. "Well, Son, how did it go?" I asked.

He looked disconsolate. "Dad, I asked her all those questions one after the other in the first five minutes, and then I didn't know what to say the rest of the night!" *Okay, Son, let's go over this again...*

Do not underestimate the importance of this kind of teaching. It gives our kids confidence and makes life more fun when they don't feel like complete klutzes on the playground or at a party. From how to drive a car to how to respond to teasing, equip them to handle life. Why else does God let us keep them for almost twenty years, if not to train them in what they need to know? That's what Dads are for!

4. Model of Masculinity

> So God created man in his own image, in the image of God he created him; male and female he created them. (Genesis 1:27)

God made us either male or female, and kids are extremely aware of the difference. One of the great issues in growing up is dealing with who you are as a boy or as a girl. From a very early age, children are busy trying to figure all of this out.

The world is so mixed up on this, it is absolutely scary. We have men wanting to be women and women wanting to be men. The superstars openly flaunt their sexual aberrations. Androgyny is the thing. You can't tell who is who or what is what without a program! The women's movement cries one thing, the gays and lesbians another; and even in our schools there is a burgeoning clamor to present homosexuality, lesbianism and cohabitation as acceptable lifestyles. Paul described it well 2000 years ago:

> Therefore God gave them over in the sinful desires of their hearts to sexual impurity for the degrading of their bodies with one another. They exchanged the truth of God for a lie, and worshiped and served created things rather than the Creator—who is forever praised. Amen. Because of this, God gave them over to shameful lusts. Even their women exchanged natural relations for unnatural ones. In the same way the men also abandoned natural relations with women and were inflamed with lust for one another. Men committed indecent acts with other men, and received in themselves the due penalty for their perversion. (Romans 1:24–27)

The challenges and problems in this area can be overwhelming. What can a father do? My answer is this: Model healthy masculinity. The real thing will outshine the twisted, warped ways of the world. Your kids will see you and know who, and what, a real man is, and what sexuality is all about.

In spite of what the world around us may say, the Bible teaches that homosexuality is both sinful and unnatural. No young boy was made that way by God. Some young men experience more temptations in this direction than others do, but the same is true for other sins as well. In my counseling experience, I have found that it is often the exploiting of the young, the weak and the naive by predatory older males that creates a homosexual. A great relationship with a strong, affectionate father reduces to virtually zero the chances for a boy to fall into this pit.

What about the son who is shy, withdrawn or effeminate,

one who is a bit of a "mama's boy" or a "sissy"? This special young boy needs to be drawn into a close relationship with his father. Give him plenty of your time and attention. Don't over-react. Don't disdain or ridicule him, and by all means don't reject him.

On the other hand, it is also important that you not ignore a persistent issue, just hoping that it will go away. Encourage and train him how to be manly. Help him with the soft lisp and girlish giggle. Teach him to relate confidently to other boys— don't let him hang out mostly with girls just because it is easier.

Help him to relate and function adequately in sports, and equip him with some manly skills. Don't force him into a strict macho mold; if he is predominantly musically or artistically inclined and is not drawn to sports, there is nothing wrong with that. Simply encourage a masculine expression of his particular gifts. And, be sure to guard him from exploitation by any other male who would take advantage of him.

Such a bonding between father and son will have a powerful effect. Your son will gain confidence. He will not feel different or weird, and he will not retreat from the legitimate male world. If he experiences the temptation of homosexual sin, he will have a much stronger ability to resist. By having a confident and close relationship with his own father, he will be less needy of an arti-ficial sense of approval from other men.

Daughters likewise need a strong, affectionate father. Such a relationship gives them security. They love the sense of approval and love that comes from a special closeness with their dad. If you are kind, strong and close to your daughter, she will want to marry someone like you. She will not be as likely to seek fulfill-ment from sexual escapades with boys who want to take advan-tage of her insecurities. She will not need to say "yes" sexually to prove anything to anyone. And she will one day make some-one a wonderful wife!

5. With Liberty and Justice for All

> The boys grew up, and Esau became a skillful hunter, a man
> of the open country, while Jacob was a quiet man, staying
> among the tents. Isaac, who had a taste for wild game,
> loved Esau, but Rebekah loved Jacob. (Genesis 25:27–28)

> When his brothers saw that their father loved him more
> than any of them, they hated him and could not speak a
> kind word to him. (Genesis 37:4)

> Acquitting the guilty and condemning the innocent—
> the LORD detests them both. (Proverbs 17:15)

As the leader, we fathers must see that there is respect given
to all, and we must rule justly in any areas of dispute. Playing
favorites is deadly. Look at the years of pain and suffering in the
families of Isaac and Jacob, brought on by the folly of parental
favoritism.

Who must be respected?

Mother

Sometimes in families with strong fathers, the children may
look upon their mother as weak in comparison to their dad. And
as children get older, the problem may worsen. Both sons and
daughters need to know that we absolutely respect our wives,
and that we expect them to honor her. We as fathers can become
party to the problem if we engage in any criticism or teasing
which degrades our wives. I can recall several moments in our
family life where I called the family together and asked for forgiveness when I felt I had been less than respectful of Geri. As
leader of our families, we need to lead the way in assuring that
our wives are given the honor that they deserve.

Younger or weaker children

Our third child Jonathan was born into a family inhabited by a strong, opinionated older sister and brother. They were quick with an answer, and they spoke out freely. As Jonathan grew, we had to make room for him in conversation. At the dinner table, while he was trying to get his sentences figured out, the conversation had long since moved to other subjects. And when he did try to speak, his older siblings helped him out by finishing his sentences for him!

Geri noticed Jonathan's growing frustration and pointed it out to me. We talked about it in our family devotional time and decided to give Jonathan the floor whenever he wanted it—all he had to do was raise his hand. It worked. So well, in fact, that Jonathan started putting his hand up too much!

When Alexandra came along, almost six years younger than the next in line, we had to go through this again. She would not sit, as did Jonathan, and let her frustrations build. Oh, no! She would speak right up in the middle of someone else's sentence, on a completely different subject. Tension was building and feelings were getting hurt. Once again, I had to act to secure everyone's rights.

These may seem to be trivial issues, but they are not. In the life of a child, they are huge. As kids get older, the issues become obviously more critical. But your role as dispenser of justice starts from Day One, and it is one of your most vital roles. (See chapters 5 and 9 for more discussion on respect and harmony among children.)

Part 2

The Father As Lover

Authority without love creates fear and rebellion. If we want to raise awesome kids, we need to lead and love. The combination is powerful and will bond us to our children for life.

1. Compassion and Caring

> The LORD is compassionate and gracious,
>   slow to anger, abounding in love.
> He will not always accuse,
>   nor will he harbor his anger forever;
> he does not treat us as our sins deserve
>   or repay us according to our iniquities.
> For as high as the heavens are above the earth,
>   so great is his love for those who fear him;
> as far as the east is from the west,
>   so far has he removed our transgressions from us.
> As a father has compassion on his children,
>   so the LORD has compassion on those who fear him;
> for he knows how we are formed,
>   he remembers that we are dust. (Psalm 103:8–14)

Fatherly Care

God cares. He is aware of our needs, our feelings, our problems, and he is concerned. There is nothing too great or too small to escape his notice or to be beneath or beyond his love.

Fathers, we need to imitate this caring. We must take notice of our children. Are they happy? Sad? Worried? Burdened? We need to watch their eyes, listen to their words, and watch their body language. Our care should flow out as a healthy, refreshing stream. We ought to be a fountainhead of love and concern for our wives and children and be available to meet a need whatever it is and whenever it arises.

Many of us are oblivious to our children's needs. They are going through struggles with homework, schoolmates and a myriad of other things, and we aren't tuned in. They feel distant from us. We are up in the clouds, consumed with work or our own problems. They may drop hints or say something in passing that should alert us.

Sometimes our wives will see something wrong with the kids and try to tell us, but we aren't listening, and the opportunity passes us by.

The day will come when our children will go to someone else because they have given up trying to reach us. They will have no desire to talk to us anymore. Our hearts will break, and we will wonder, "Why can't I reach my kids?" The reason is that we weren't there when they reached for us.

Fatherly Compassion

Not only caring for, but *feeling with*, is the way a father loves. It is a great comfort to know that God hurts for us and with us. He feels what we feel. He is not coldly logical. His great heart goes out to us:

> "But while he was still a long way off, his father saw him and was filled with compassion for him; he ran to his son, threw his arms around him and kissed him." (Luke 15:20)

We need to put ourselves in our children's shoes, to remember what it was like to be a kid. Many children's problems are solved simply by them knowing that we feel with them and for them.

Fatherly Forgiveness

When children have done wrong, they need to ask our forgiveness, and we need to grant it. They need to know that they are forgiven and that there is no cloud hanging over their heads.

Let them know that it is over and done with. We should not put our children in the doghouse of disapproval, where they feel they never quite have our blessing.

Fatherly Understanding

> ...for he knows how we are formed,
> he remembers that we are dust. (Psalm 103:14)

Our children are...children! Give them time to grow up. Let them be kids. They are young, immature, weak, clumsy and foolish. They sneeze, snort, stink, slip, stumble and snicker. We should expect a lot, but we must make wise allowance for immaturity. The world has enough proper, pompous, sanitized adults to go around. Remember—God is patient with us!

2. Encouragement and Inspiration

> You know that we dealt with each of you as a father deals with his own children, encouraging, comforting, and urging you to live lives worthy of God, who calls you into his kingdom and glory. (1 Thessalonians 2:11–12)

Life is hard. It is especially hard for kids. They get plenty of ridicule, teasing and "nyah nyah nyahs" from their peers. It is easy to lose heart. How many kids could accomplish so much more but fail because no one is there to encourage or inspire them?

There is immense power in a father's encouragement. There is a mystical, almost magical energy unleashed when Dad says, "You can do it."

Young Timothy was well spoken of by the church (Acts 16:2) but he had weaknesses. He lacked confidence (2 Timothy 1:8, 1 Corinthians 16:10), could lose motivation (2 Timothy 1:6-7), got ill frequently (1 Timothy 5:23), and tended to be lazy (1 Timothy 4:13-15). This young man possessed talent, conviction and heart, but needed someone to believe in him and train him. Apparently, he had never had a strong male spiritual influence (Acts 16:1, 2 Timothy 1:5).

Paul met Timothy and took him into his heart and under his wing. He became his "father in the faith" (1 Corinthians 4:17). By his encouragement and inspiration he helped turned this underachieving young man into the dynamic leader of the church in Ephesus.

Have great vision for your children. Encourage them unceasingly as they struggle to learn and accomplish. Pressure doesn't work, but inspiration does. And nothing is more inspiring to children than their father's belief in them.

One of our jobs as fathers is to wisely and soberly assess our children's gifts and talents and direct them into areas where they can excel. Some kids are frustrated because they are trying to succeed in a field in which they are not gifted. Don't let them spin their wheels. Give wise counsel, and be patient with each child as he or she finds their way to those activities and projects at which they can be fulfilled and successful.

I coached my boys' soccer teams for four years. On my rosters I had everyone from superstars to guys who could barely kick the ball. My job was to believe in and inspire every player and to give each one a sense of his importance to our team. I had to find each player's best position, where his strengths were maximized and his weaknesses were minimized.

There were coaches in our league who just put their boys out in a big mass on the field and let them play. Some coaches "led" by cursing, screaming and berating their players. Others put all their efforts into one or two great athletes, depending on them to carry the team.

My assistants and I coached every player to the maximum of his potential. We accepted them where they were and took them

44

higher. We encouraged each boy as he improved.

They loved it, and they had fun. Each one had a place, felt important, and improved as a player and as a person. In those four years, we won two championships and were in the playoffs the other two times. It was not that we had teams stacked with talent. It was that we got the most out of all sixteen players.

My challenge to fathers is this: be the great inspirer and encourager of your children. Don't push them to be winners or stars to meet some need within yourself. Teach them to be good sports, to work hard and to learn how to win and how to lose. Let it be you who thinks they are great and who picks them up when they fall. They will love you for it, and their gratitude and accomplishments will be your reward.

3. Humility and Approachability

> All of you, clothe yourselves with humility toward one another, because, "God opposes the proud but gives grace to the humble." (1 Peter 5:5)

Our families know assuredly that we are imperfect; we might as well admit it. Let's take off the mask of superiority and stop pretending that we are always right. I have found that since I bear the most responsibility in my house, then I make the most mistakes. I have often said, "No one in my house apologizes more than I do." If we are quick to demand apologies but rarely or reluctantly give them, we set up everyone for resentment.

Strong leadership, to some of us, means creating a mystique of infallibility. We feel that to reveal weakness would cause in our followers a loss of confidence and respect. The most powerful and endearing leaders I know are men and women without pretension. Like Paul, they say, "I am the chief of sinners." When they admit their weaknesses and are honest about their struggles, I only admire them more.

Apologize clearly and specifically. If you were angry and harsh, go to your children and say, "I am sorry. I spoke harshly to you. That is not the way Dad should speak. Please forgive me."

Apologize quickly. This prevents hurt feelings from degenerating into anger, sullenness and bitterness.

Afterwards, make sure the air is clear. Ask, "Is everything all right? Is anything else bothering you?" Remember: because you are an authority figure, they may not feel free to say everything on their mind. Help them to get it all out.

In raising my own children I relied on my wife to help me see my errors with the kids. Sometimes I did not realize a hurt I caused. Geri would sense that something was wrong, or the children would bring it to her attention. She would then send them to me or bring it up to me herself. I was thankful for these talks, although sometimes at first my defenses went up.

Once the apologies are made and the relationship is repaired, then the issue is closed. We are free to lead again. We should move forward confidently, knowing that under God, all is well. Wallowing in guilt or losing confidence over our mistakes does not help our families. Nor is it true humility; it is a lack of faith in God's grace. Our families need our hand firmly back on the helm, and quickly.

The stronger men and leaders we are, the more we will need to cultivate the quality of approachability. People in our families should feel free to come to us and tell us whatever is on their minds, be it embarrassing, negative or difficult. If we blow up in anger or will not listen, then we are unapproachable.

To express something negative does not necessarily mean a child has a bad attitude; to fail to express it at all will certainly create one! Never should we put our family members in this position. It is our responsibility as the leader to create a feeling of freedom and openness in our households. If we do not, we are headed for a day of bitter reckoning.

I have been amazed at some of the things my kids needed to discuss with me, but were afraid to bring up. The subjects ranged from guilt over past misdeeds (some of which seemed trivial to me) to their current struggles with the most serious temptations. They brought me their questions, problems and insecurities. We talked them all out. I wanted my children to know that as a godly father I would tell them the truth and uphold God's standards; but I also wanted them to know that they could talk to me about anything, and I would listen.

4. Have Fun, Be Hip

What's wrong with having fun? What's unspiritual about laughing until you fall out of your chair? Absolutely nothing! Holiness makes for happiness. The Committed can clown around sometimes. M. Scott Peck is right when he says, "Saints must sleep and prophets must play."[2]

Jesus was a fun person. He went to parties. He told jokes. He nicknamed his guys ("Rocky" and "Sons of Thunder"). He loved children, and they loved him.

The Pharisees were so uptight they drove people out of the kingdom. They even rebuked Jesus for letting his disciples get too happy. Jesus did not let these grumps have their way. He responded: "If they keep quiet, the stones will cry out" (Luke 19:40).

Children love fun people. We can always be serious when need be. It is simply a matter of knowing what mood to set. If Dad, the leader, can tell (or take) a joke, everybody has fun. Sometimes, after a hard day, everybody just needs to laugh and kick back. If we are fun people, and let our kids have fun, they will love our leadership.

Fathers need to be in tune with the current scene. You don't

---

2. M. Scott Peck, *The Road Less Traveled* (New York: Touchstone Publishers, 1978), 107.

have to be a goof-ball older guy trying to be young (please, spare us!), but you do need to be hip to what's happening. Out-of-touch fathers are unconnected to their children. If you are this way, then your kid has to make one of several decisions, all bad: (1) humor my father but hide him from my friends, (2) become out of touch myself, (3) relate to my dad superficially since he is clueless about my real life.

We show love when we are interested in someone else's world. It demonstrates that we care enough to get inside their feelings and experiences. Paul said, "I have become all things to all men so that by all possible means I might save some" (1 Corinthians 9:22). If we are going to save our kids, then we need to connect with, and not just ridicule, the current youth scene. Try to understand the music, the lingo and the clothes. You can accept the style and still confront the sin. And, it helps when we remember what we felt and did when we were that age.

I began this chapter by sharing with you my relationship with my father. I carry his memory in my heart and have his picture on my desk. I hold as one of my prize possessions the shotgun he presented me as he lay upon his deathbed.

I have often longed for a chance to see him again, for a time to sit and talk, to tell him all I feel, and to let him see who I have become. I have also wished that I could listen to him and come to know him as I never did. And I am not alone in my feelings. I have spoken to many other men who feel the same way.

But while we cannot relive our past, we can build a better future. We can be to our children the father that we wish we could have had. We can give them our loving leadership, knowing that this is one of the most precious gifts we can ever give, and that our children can ever receive.

Chapter 3

Wife and Mother

A wife of noble character who can find?
She is worth far more than rubies....
Her children arise and call her blessed;
her husband also, and he praises her,
"Many women do noble things,
but you surpass them all."

Proverbs 31:10, 28–29

What is your concept of the ideal wife and mother? It used to be so much clearer and more easily understood. However, as women have become "liberated" and life has become more fast-paced, traditional moral values and roles within the family have been questioned, ridiculed and all but disregarded. We desire to have great families, yet we are walking along paths that are no longer clearly defined.

So how can we understand the woman's role in marriage and motherhood, and where do we start? God has actually defined it rather simply. In almost every scripture referring to the role of the wife, God comes back to the basic principle of submission and adaptation. (Yes, there it is...the hated word—"submission"!) And when the Bible discusses motherhood, it defines that role primarily as one of nurturing.

Some of us are good mothers, yet we leave much to be

49

desired as wives. Others of us are devoted wives, but are inadequate mothers. Both of these roles must be fulfilled as God intended in order to have a happy, harmonious family life and to raise well-adjusted children.

In my experience, I have found that more women fail as supportive wives than as nurturing mothers. Most problems in family life are the result of difficulties in the marriage. We can be the world's most wonderful mother, but if we are filled with selfishness and bitterness as a wife, our children will suffer, and their lives will bear the consequences of our sin!

First, we will look at and discuss the role of submission in marriage and see how this affects our ability to be effective mothers.

Part 1

The Wife—Model of Submission

Wives, submit to your husbands as to the Lord.... Now as the church submits to Christ, so also wives should submit to their husbands in everything. (Ephesians 5:22, 24)

Wives, submit to your husbands as is fitting in the Lord. (Colossians 3:18)

Wives, in the same way be submissive to your husbands...like Sarah, who obeyed Abraham and called him her master. You are her daughters if you do what is right and do not give way to fear. (1 Peter 3:1, 5–6)

Then they can train the younger women to love their husbands and children, to be self-controlled and pure, to be busy at home, to be kind, and to be subject to their husbands, so that no one will malign the word of God. (Titus 2:4–5)

The ability to adapt and adjust to authority is one of the most important lessons we must learn in life. Rebellion against God's authority resulted in Satan being cast out of heaven (Revelation 12:7-9) and Adam and Eve being cast out of the Garden (Genesis 3:23). Not only must we submit to God, but to numerous other authorities—the government, employers, parents, teachers and coaches, to name just a few.

God uses the family unit to demonstrate and model the principles of life that all of us must learn. By God's design so much of life is encompassed and acted out at home—leadership, respect, obedience, love, encouragement and the give-and-take in relationships. Get it right at home, and we will probably get it right everywhere else!

God's plan is for the husband to lead with power and humility and for the wife to follow with strength and support. The wife has the very unique role of modeling in the flesh the role of submission, a role her children must learn if they are to succeed in life. How many children never learn to submit to legitimate authorities because they never see a healthy example at home?

My mother modeled submission for me as a child in a way more powerful than words could ever describe. It was obvious by what she said and how she said it that she deeply respected my father. I always knew that once my dad had made a decision, there would be no arguing, complaining or maneuvering around it.

Because of the submission my mother demonstrated, I grew up with a healthy respect for men and other authorities and with a positive view of marriage as well.

Why have we reacted so negatively to the idea of submission? For most of us, it is because submission implies weakness and wimpiness. Unfortunately, that is often the way we have seen it applied. We have seen women who are beaten down, anxious, fearful and lacking any sense of self-esteem or self-confidence, and we have concluded that these traits are a result of submission.

Nothing could be further from the truth. The word "submissive" is not and was never intended to be synonymous with "weak." Look at the examples of godly, submissive women in the Bible—they are anything but weak! Consider Sarah, Rebekah, Deborah, Abigail, Mary the mother of Jesus, Priscilla and the noble woman of Proverbs 31. These are women with passion, spunk and sparkle. They exemplify undaunted courage and strong convictions, and yet, their lives exude a spirit of submission.

Now, let's get practical. What does it mean then to "submit," and how does a wife serve as a model of the submissive spirit to her children? Let us look at three different aspects of submission.

1. Submission: An Ordering of Relationships

People of all ages function best when the order of relationships is clearly defined. While many of us would always like to be the one in charge, life goes smoothly only when it is clearly established who is in charge and who will follow. This is true in the classroom, in business and at home.

I remember one day when our oldest daughter was three and a half, she looked at me with the "Aha!" look that a child gets when he or she finally understands an important truth. She said, "I know! God is the boss of Daddy; Daddy is the boss of you; you are the boss of me...and I am the boss of Sunny [our twenty-five-pound dog]!"

Yes, life works better when we understand the order of relationships! This is God's way of doing things, and we mothers need to demonstrate it practically to our children.

2. Submission: More an Attitude Than an Action

...and the wife must respect her husband. (Ephesians 5:33)

This concept must be grasped in order to understand submission. Submission is an attitude of respect that issues from our hearts. How many of us have seen and been repulsed by women who do all the right things and yet are obviously seething with anger and disdain for their husbands?

Let me ask, what does this attitude produce in the children who are watching? It produces children who begrudgingly do as they are told, but with sullenness, defiance and deceitfulness.

Respectful submission is only possible if we have the proper attitude about ourselves. "Do not think of yourselves more highly than you ought, but rather think of yourself with sober judgment" (Romans 12:3). Let's face it: most of us have a problem with submission because we are sure that we are right! Submission is usually not an issue until there is a disagreement or a difference of opinion. Think about it—if both of you were in agreement, would there be a submission issue?

Obviously, none of us can ever compromise the will and commands of God under the guise of being submissive. Our obedience to God takes absolute precedence over any other authority in life. "We must obey God rather than men" (Acts 5:29). But, there are, and always will be, times when one of us must yield to the other. Submission does not mean we have no opinions. (I personally have opinions about almost everything!) It does mean that we are not always right and that there will be times when we willingly yield our opinions or our desires or our way of doing something to our husband's.

We must do this without resentment and without self-pity. We must submit without thinking, "I hope he's wrong," and without saying, "I told you so!" if, in fact, we prove to be right.

Why is this so important in parenting? Have you ever dealt with a child who fully believed he or she was right or with a teenager who was convinced he or she knew everything there was to know about life? As parents, we expect our children to obey and to yield to our decisions. How much easier it is for a child or a teenager to submit when they have seen that attitude continually modeled by their parents.

Submission is not a technique that we use to resolve conflict; it is a basic attitude of respect. A submissive spirit is more than a mere acquiescence in order to keep peace; it is a way of valuing our husbands. When a woman respects her husband it is obvious. He feels it; the children see and imitate it, and all the world takes notice!

3. Submission: A Way of Speaking

> If anyone considers himself religious and yet does not keep a tight rein on his tongue, he deceives himself and his religion is worthless. (James 1:26)

> The tongue is a fire, a world of evil among the parts of the body. It corrupts the whole person, sets the whole course of his life on fire, and is itself set on fire by hell. (James 3:6)

Words have an amazing power—power to build up or power to destroy. They can be precious gifts or hurtful weapons. How many times have we heard words flying from our mouths—words that we could not seem to stop, words that were destined to ridicule, hurt, tear down or threaten?

Once released, they sped toward the target, free to wound and damage. We can apologize and repent afterwards, but unwise, hurtful words cannot be ignored, recaptured or ever quite forgotten.

As wives and mothers we must carefully guard our speech.

We must use our words to bring about good, not harm. Nowhere is a submissive spirit demonstrated more powerfully than in the way a woman uses her words.

One of my favorite women in the Bible is Abigail (1 Samuel 25). While I admire Abigail's courage and tenacity, she especially serves as a model of how to say difficult things in the right way. Submission does not always mean silence. Abigail confronted David directly, and yet, she did it with the utmost respect and concern. She exemplifies "speaking the truth in love" (Ephesians 4:15), showing us that anything that needs to be said can be said when it is spoken in the right way.

In every family there will be times when we must talk through difficult issues. As husbands and wives, we must learn to talk with one another and even to challenge one another, yet be mindful that we are on the same side.

We must speak candidly and yet with genuine love and respect. Never is there an excuse to belittle or berate each other or to speak to each other with crudeness and cursing. These are the words that kill marriages, destroy lives and ruin children! If our words are spoken with love and respect, we can say whatever must be said, solve any problem, and come out united. Just as David owed Abigail his very soul because of the things she courageously said to him, so will we help each other stay saved and make it to heaven. What greater lessons can our children learn than how to talk about difficult things openly, honestly and respectfully?

It is said of the noble woman of Proverbs 31 that "she speaks with wisdom, and faithful instruction is on her tongue" (v26). As a result, her children and her husband praise her (v28). But of another woman in Proverbs it is said, "Better to live in a desert than with a quarrelsome and ill-tempered wife" (Proverbs 21:19).

Which is the best description of your conversation? Is it wise and faithful or quarrelsome and ill-tempered? Nothing destroys the atmosphere of a home more than a whining, contradictory wife. A negative, complaining atmosphere robs a family of joy and peace. This kind of talk is also contagious! Do your children whine, complain, argue? Could it be they are only imitating what they see in you?

The atmosphere and tone of the home rests with you, and much of it is determined by the way you speak—first, to your husband, and second, to your children.

Part 2

The Mother As Nurturer

...but his mother treasured all these things in her heart. And Jesus grew in wisdom and stature, and in favor with God and men. (Luke 2:51–52)

Just as Jesus was loved and cared for by his mother, we also must love and take care of our children. Our primary role as mother is one of nurturer. We will discuss the four main ways we must nurture our children: emotionally, physically, spiritually and socially.

1. Nurture Them Emotionally

As a mother comforts her child,
so will I comfort you. (Isaiah 66:13)

We were gentle among you like a mother caring for her little children. (1 Thessalonians 2:7)

The entire world can be against us; life can be incredibly difficult, but all is well in those moments when we feel a mother's love! There is nothing quite like it! It is God's plan for the comfort and closeness of a mother's love to be our initial taste of this world. It is the first relationship of love that a person experiences in this life, and it prepares us for life ahead.

A special closeness

Most of us deeply love our children and, in the early months, are especially close to them. We feed them, cuddle them and meet their every need. Yet, as those babies grow older, we can lose the special closeness of infancy. An intimate relationship with our children must continually be cultivated. This relationship will convince them that they are valuable human beings even when the world tries to make them feel worthless. It will serve as a solid bulwark against the inevitable ups and downs of life as they make their way out into the world.

Learn how to be a warm, affectionate person. Touch your children, hug them, smile at them, encourage them with your words. Tell them over and over again how much you love them! I often said to Alexandra, my youngest, "Do you know how much I love you?"

She would always answer with the same words that I had spoken so many times to her: "More than all the world and everything that is in it!"

I realized long ago, as we first began to raise our children, how very much I did not know and how many times I made mistakes. I held on to a scripture then and still rely on it today (especially as our children became teenagers!): "Above all, love each other deeply, because love covers a multitude of sins" (1 Peter 4:8).

I decided then: I will probably make plenty of mistakes, but my children will never doubt how much I love them and believe in them. I am sure that my love has protected them many times from my imperfections as a parent!

A special relationship

Not only must there be the emotional bond of love and affection with our children, but there must be a unique relationship with each of them as individuals.

Every child is a unique creation of God. He broke the mold after making each one. Each of your children must hold a very special place in your heart that can be filled by no one else. What if God loved us deeply, but only en masse? Thankfully, he loves us individually. Each of us has a special place in his heart. He knows us, loves us, and "likes" us. He knows the number of hairs on our heads and has our own room in heaven prepared especially for us.

I thought for years that I was my mother's favorite daughter until as an adult I discovered that all three of my sisters were convinced of the same thing about themselves. It was not that my mother told any one of us that she was loved more than the others. No, it was just the way she loved us as individuals and made all of us feel uniquely valued and appreciated. We all grew up believing we were special and knowing we were deeply loved. Now that is the work of a great mother!

From oldest to youngest, from similar personalities to exact opposites, our children must feel bonded in heart to us. In one sense, we must love each of them "the most" because each adds something to our lives that no one else does. The more children you have and the busier life becomes, the more difficult this will be.

Our family experienced a wake-up call in this area with our youngest child. The first three of our children were born fairly close together and our fourth, Alexandra, followed six years later. By the time Alexandra was born, the other children were busy in school, and I had begun working full time in the ministry.

Because of the demands on our schedule, we hired someone to help us at home. Although I thoroughly enjoyed Alexandra, I did not realize until several years later that I was not as close to her emotionally (nor she to me) as I had been to the others.

We eventually moved and the person whom Alexandra had come to love so much no longer worked for us. The weakness in our relationship was exposed. Alexandra changed from an active, joyful toddler to a quiet little girl. She cried easily and no longer enjoyed school. I checked everything—her health, her school, her friends, her schedule. None of those things was the problem.

Finally, Sam said he felt the problem was that she just did not feel close to me! After dealing with my guilt, regret and pride, I went to work on my relationship with Alexandra. I spent more time with her, talked more to her, and listened attentively when she talked to me. (It is so easy not to be attentive to a four-year-old when you have three older children clamoring to talk about seemingly more important things!) I am happy to say that the improvements in her behavior came quickly and were dramatic.

I am so thankful that the problem was exposed as it was and when it was. It frightens me to think of the direction Alexandra's life could have taken, as well as the relationship and friendship with her that might never have been mine, had this not changed.

She is a precious gift from God and today, as a beautiful young woman, she sparkles with love and a joyful zest for life. More than loving her, I am close to her. I know her, and I like her. She has a strong will that required a firm hand, but we built the relationship needed to take her through childhood and on into life!

A special understanding

Without an understanding of our children as individuals, it is impossible to train and mold them adequately. Too many parents love their children but honestly do not know or understand them. How can you "train a child in the way he should go" (Proverbs 22:6) when you do not know where he or she is coming from?

God, the perfect example of parenthood, loves us and knows us, intimately and individually.

> Oh LORD, you have searched me
> and you know me.
> You know when I sit and when I rise;
> You perceive my thoughts from afar.
> You discern my going out and my lying down;
> You are familiar with all my ways.
> Before a word is on my tongue
> you know it completely, O LORD.
> Where can I go from your Spirit?
> Where can I flee from your presence?
> Even there your hand will guide me,
> your right hand will hold me fast.
> (Psalm 139:1–4, 7, 10)

Mothers, study your children. Discover their abilities and talents and learn their character strengths. Build up, encourage and develop these areas of their lives.

What are their weaknesses? Are there weaknesses of ability or proficiency that you can help strengthen? What are their character flaws that if left unaddressed will destroy them as adults? Is there laziness, deceitfulness, selfishness, uncontrolled anger?

If we would only nurture our children's characters as zealously as we encourage their mental capacities and athletic abilities, we would raise awesome kids.

I don't understand it—maybe it comes from the nine months of pregnancy in which we shared the same body; perhaps it is women's intuition; maybe it is just the enhanced sensitivity that is a part of love. But I do believe God gives mothers a unique ability to sense the needs and to draw out the feelings of children. We may be the one who first senses hurt feelings, anger or bad attitudes. We also may be the first to realize that there is a more serious problem. Mothers, we must watch, listen, pay attention and deal with what we see.

On the other hand, never undermine your children's relationship with their dad. Often it is easier to talk to Mom. We may seem softer and less intimidating, or perhaps we see needs more quickly. This is understandable, but it should never lead to a situation where Mom and the kids are close and talk freely, but Dad is kept in the dark.

Encourage and insist that your children learn to talk to their father, especially as they get older. In our family, the children have a very healthy respect for their dad. They love and admire Sam greatly, yet sometimes they were afraid of what he would say or think. Especially when they were younger, it was sometimes easier for them to come to me. I worked very hard to help them feel free to talk to their father and never allowed myself to be in the middle of a strained or awkward relationship.

It takes work to nurture your children emotionally. Some of you may be feeling quite overwhelmed. Let me give you some practical advice that can help:

• Make use of the little periods of time. Throughout the day, grasp the minutes here and there to talk with and draw near to your children. As they get older, this will be even more important because small amounts of time will often be all you will have.

• Take one with you! Ever since our third child was born and we were outnumbered by children, Sam and I made it our practice to take a child with us whenever possible as we ran errands. Instead of being "dead" time, grocery shopping, banking, etc. can be spent enjoying the company of our children.

• Consider chauffeuring a blessing from God! I sometimes thought that I should put my entire house on wheels since I seemed to be living in the car, chauffeuring children to and from school and countless activities. If we let it, this can be one of the most frustrating parts of motherhood. We are always in the car!

Yet, we probably should count it as one of God's real blessings to our lives. The time I spent in the car each day provided some of the best time to talk with our older children. Not only did it allow us to talk about things they were troubled by, tempted with or excited about, but it gave me the chance to give guidance and input to situations just as they got ready to meet them. I would often drop them off and pray all the way home about the things I had just heard! Also, driving them places with their friends enabled me to overhear conversations and understand the mindset of other kids.

• Make bedtimes special. Spend a few minutes at bedtime talking about the day. Sometimes children need to talk about their feelings—hurt, disappointment, anger, joy. At other times they need to confess sins and clear their consciences before us and before God. (All of us know how much better is the sleep of a clear conscience!) And at every bedtime, love can be expressed with words and with touch; whether it be hugs and kisses or a light caress, a gentle squeeze or a loving pat. The last thing I wanted my children to know before they closed their eyes at night was that I loved them with all my heart.

2. Nurture Them Physically

> She is like the merchant ships,
>   bringing her food from afar.
> She gets up while it is still dark;
>   she provides food for her family

and portions for her servant girls.
When it snows, she has no fear for her household;
for all of them are clothed in scarlet.
She makes coverings for her bed;
she is clothed in fine linen and purple.
(Proverbs 31:14–15, 21–22)

As do all mothers, I cherish every card, letter and hand-made gift my children have given to me. Their expressions of devotion move me to tears and also bring smiles to my face. The things they thank us for are the things that are most important to them.

I am reminded of a card that Jonathan wrote to me for Valentine's Day when he was about eight years old. I share with you just as he wrote it,

> Who knows where the family'd be without you?
> We'd have bad food, always be late for school,
> unhappy. We'd be a mess!

So much of nurturing a child is providing for his or her physical needs. It takes an incredible amount of time and energy to run a household and take care of our families. On top of all of this, many of us mothers are juggling a full-time job outside the home. Regardless of how demanding our jobs are or how busy our schedules, if we have children, then we must take care of them!

Children need to be fed decent, nourishing meals at regular times. (In a later chapter we will deal more with the importance of eating meals together as a family.) Some of us are so busy that our meals too often consist of snacks or fast-food stops. There is nothing wrong with occasionally eating pizza or fast-food hamburgers. But as mothers we are given the job of providing nourishing meals for our families, and we need to do it.

We do not need to be short-order cooks, preparing a different meal for every family member according to his or her taste or desire that particular day. Children are often picky eaters. The best way to handle "pickiness" is to not make it a big deal. I always tried to have at least one thing I knew a picky eater would like. If they ate only that one thing but nothing else, I did not expect anything more than that they try one taste of the other things. I did not go back to the stove preparing two or three other tasty treats for the one with the delicate taste buds.

I have seen mothers worrying so much over what their little ones were or were not eating that they actually created an eating problem! Most children get what they need as long as we don't fill them up with junk food.

Young children will have meals where they eat some foods and hardly touch others. David, my most finicky eater when he was young, usually ate everything in sight at breakfast, a small amount of lunch and almost nothing at dinner. He loved white rice, so I prepared many meals with that on the menu. We chose not overreact to David's unusual culinary preferences, and needless to say, our son lived and grew. Eventually, he ate more than anyone else in our family!

On the other hand, undisciplined eating creates problems that can last into adulthood. Growing children may need snacks several times a day in addition to regular nutritious meals, but they should not eat uncontrollably or indiscriminately.

In our family, we never allowed our children unlimited access to snack foods. They were not free to "graze" through the kitchen all day long. Too many children are overweight and physically unfit. Often these same children struggle with a weak, self-indulgent character. Help them while they are young to establish disciplined eating habits and healthy attitudes about food.

Aside from the challenges of feeding a growing family, our job is to make sure our children are clothed properly. This can be quite a challenge, both to our schedules and to our bank accounts. I can remember the expense of buying four pairs of shoes at the beginning of the school year. The older and bigger the children (and their feet) got, the more expensive the shoes! We must have a godly focus on the physical needs of life, and women, especially, must keep a balanced perspective. Because we are the ones who take care of so many of the physical needs of our families, we spend more time in the stores and are confronted with the glitz and glamour of things. The physical needs of life are legitimate and important, but they must never become our focus or take the place of the things that really matter.

Mothers, our attitudes on these things will be imitated by our children. If we are consumed with external appearances and material things, they will be also! If our attitudes are healthy and spiritual, these same attitudes will be reflected in our children.

> "...Is not life more important than...clothes? ...So do not worry saying, 'What shall we eat?' or 'What shall we wear?' For the pagans run after all these things, and your heavenly Father knows that you need them. But seek first his kingdom and his righteousness and all of these things will be given to you as well." (Matthew 6:25, 31–33)

Now that I've said all of this, let me say that it is important to help our children dress and carry themselves in such a way as to relate with and be accepted by other people, especially their peers. Some children are more concerned with their appearance than others. As a teacher, I know that the neatness, cleanliness and attractiveness of children does affect their behavior and, like it or not, the way they are treated by their teachers and their peers.

If your children have no idea what looks good, help them. Just make sure your own ideas of what is attractive are coming out of today and not the 1980s! I remember speaking with a mother concerning her twelve-year-old son. He was often ridiculed by other kids. He was called names and put down repeatedly on the bus and at school.

As I got to know this boy, I realized that he had a great heart and a likeable personality, but it was difficult to get past his appearance. He always looked sloppy, out-dated and slightly effeminate. While some of us could see beyond this and like him as a person, the children at school (and many adults as well) were never going to give this kid a chance.

I spoke to his mother about getting him a professional hair cut (Mom had been his barber) and helping him dress better. He showed up at church several days later with a new hair cut and "lookin' good"! He obviously felt like a new man!

Mothers, you do not have to spend large amounts of money or dress your children like models, but it is your job to help them look good and be relatable. Appearance is only external, but it is the first thing people see. If we fail to dress our children within reasonable limits of fashion and neatness, we do our children a grave disservice.

Let me say one more thing regarding physical needs and appearance. It matters to children how their parents look. They want to be proud of us when they introduce us to their friends or, heaven forbid, when they are seen with us! As I said earlier, we do not have to become obsessed with our appearances, but we do need to do the best we can with what we've got.

Mothers, as we get older, we will have to put some effort into staying in shape (or getting there to begin with!). We will not only look better, but will have more energy. It is my observation that if we judiciously put on make-up, style our hair, and dress attractively, we will have a better attitude about life and our children will have a better attitude about us.

3. Nurture Them Spiritually

When our children are small, we probably will be the primary person to demonstrate and teach them a genuine, live faith. We usually spend more time with young children, especially if we are able to be at home with them.

Beginning when they are very young, we can teach our children that God loves them, and we can help them to love him back. "We love God because he first loved us" (1 John 4:19). Love for God begins with a heart-felt appreciation for all that he is, all he has done and all he has given. Gratitude does not necessarily come naturally to children—it must be taught and explained.

Chapter 7 will be devoted to the spiritual training of children, but let me discuss a few specifics for mothers of younger children:

Teach them to love God through nature

When was the last time you noticed the beauty of God's sunrise or sunset? When did you last marvel at the power of God in the pounding surf or at his magnificence in the vivid colors of autumn? To this day, when my own faith weakens or falters, I go back to the God I know from nature. I look around at the beauty, power and intricacy of creation, and I always come back to the same truth: only a God powerful enough to be Lord could have done all of this.

> For since the creation of the world God's invisible qualities—his eternal power and divine nature—have been clearly seen, being understood from what has been made.
> (Romans 1:20)

Help your children develop a real awareness of and love for what God has made. Show them, tell them, and teach them the magic of God's creation. I believe a child who deeply loves and appreciates what God has made will, like David of the Bible, grow up to be a man or woman after God's own heart.

Teach them by our lives

It's plain and simple—"actions speak louder than words." Our children need to see that we really believe God is our Father and that Jesus is our Savior! They need to see that we have a genuine relationship with them, and it affects every part of our lives. I remember overhearing Elizabeth, when she was quite young, tell a friend, "My mom prays a lot."

Do our children see that God is real in our lives? Do they know that we pray and talk to him? Do they see us reading the Bible and allowing God's words to guide our lives? God will be as real to our children as he is to us. If our religion is mere talk, doctrine or a harsh taskmaster, so it will be for them. Our children will not see perfect parents, but they can see mothers and fathers who sincerely love God and are doing their best to follow him.

Teach them with the Scriptures

> But as for you, continue in what you have learned and have become convinced of, because you know those from whom you learned it, and how from infancy you have known the holy Scriptures, which are able to make you wise for salvation through faith in Christ Jesus. All Scripture is God-breathed and is useful for teaching, rebuking, correcting and training in righteousness, so that the man of God may be thoroughly equipped for every good work. (2 Timothy 3:14–16)

I believe with all my heart that the Bible is from God and provides answers and guidance to any situation. I believe that when the Bible is obeyed and its principles or commands followed, they always work. But what has amazed me is the power of God's word to change my children! I said things over and over again to my children with little response and much frustration. Can you relate?

I also used the Bible to teach the very same things, and my children responded eagerly and immediately! I do not understand it except to say that the Bible is "living and active" (Hebrews 4:12) and, more than any other book, the Bible is your best resource.

It helps the children to realize that there is a standard over both of us. It is not just Mom saying to obey; God wants Mom and us to obey him. Use the Scriptures to mold character and to teach your children the truths about life! You can find a scripture or an example to help you deal with any situation, any problem, any attitude. Here are some particular situations you may need to deal with and the scriptures that we used with our children:

Jealousy – Genesis 4:4–9

At five years old, Elizabeth was quite jealous of David. One day I exasperatedly read this scripture about Cain and Abel to her, a little unsure if it might be too strong. She thought about it, looked at me and said, "I wonder if they didn't like each other when they were little?" She got it!

Sibling Relationships – Exodus 2:1–10

The story of Miriam and Moses is a great example of an older sibling taking care of a younger brother or sister.

James 4:1–2

Do you have children who are constantly quarrelling or who don't get along? The real problem is that they both want their own way.

Whining and Complaining – Philippians 4:4

This is one of the first scriptures our children memorized

when they were unhappy and whining. Again, the special power of the Scriptures: when we would begin to say this scripture and have Elizabeth say it with us, she would always burst out laughing!

Philippians 2:14–15

Encourage them to want to "shine like stars." Alexandra loved this scripture. She, like many of us, responds best when she is inspired to be better.

Worrying and Fretting – Philippians 4:6–7

This is a wonderful scripture to teach them how to deal with things that cause them anxiety.

> - pray about everything
> - be thankful

This was a favorite of David's. He was a worrier. We would talk about this scripture, memorize it, and pray for "peace in his heart."

Anger – Ephesians 4:25–27

Some children have a more emotional, volatile nature. They must learn to deal with things that bother them before their emotions get out of control. Jonathan struggled with his temper, and this scripture helped him tremendously. He learned to talk about what he was feeling instead of blowing up.

Laziness – Proverbs 6:6–8

Do you have a child who is content to watch everyone else carry the whole load? Deal with this while they are young! Be hard-line, and insist on hard work, but whenever possible, make it fun. Our motto for Jonathan was to "be a lover of hard work."

Love – 1 Corinthians 13:4–7

The most important quality in any of our lives is love. We must actively teach our children to be loving, caring people.

This is a great verse to memorize.

There are so many other scriptures that can be used power-fully to inspire our children, to build their faith, and to shape their character. Use the Bible. Let it "dwell in you richly" (Colossians 3:16) as you teach your children. Every principle of righteousness that you need to teach them and to answer their questions about life can be found in the Word. Use it!

4. Nurture Them Socially

> And Jesus grew in wisdom and in stature, and in favor with God and man. (Luke 2:52)

Jesus was the greatest man who ever lived. He accomplished great things for God, brought us salvation, and lived an amazing life. Yet part of the power of his life was his ability to relate to people.

As mothers we must teach our children the social skills that enable them to get along with people and to develop healthy, meaningful relationships. The most basic of these used to be taught and expected of all children, yet they seem to be forgotten today.

Teach good manners

- Whatever happened to the magic words, "please" and "thank you"? They still carry some magic. Teach them.
- How about "excuse me" or "pardon me"?
- Teach them how to properly introduce friends and family.
- Teach them not to interrupt when others are speaking.
- Teach them not to answer in monosyllabic grunts like "yeah," "nah," "huh" and/or "un-uh." Even a polite "yes" or "no" is better.

- Do our children know that it is respectful to offer adults, especially women, seats in a crowded room?
- Are we teaching our boys that it is still good manners to open and hold doors for women?
- Are we expecting our children to look for ways to help people when they see needs: carrying packages, assisting elderly people or helping with small children, etc.?

There are hundreds of other expressions of politeness and good manners ranging from table manners to phone etiquette. All of these demonstrate attitudes of respect and consideration to other people. Above all, we must teach our children to be courteous, helpful and to be aware of the feelings and needs of other people. This not only develops their character, but makes them much more attractive to everyone they meet.

Teach friendliness

Mothers, we must teach our children to be friendly. Teach them to greet people with warmth and smiles rather than sullen disinterest. Help them look people confidently in the eyes instead of down at their feet. Practice it together if necessary until they get it right.

Teach your children to be aware of new kids in their schools, at church and in their neighborhoods. Help them to overcome their own shyness and awkwardness and reach out to other people.

We may need to help them learn how to initiate conversations. Nothing is so awkward or embarrassing as not knowing what to say. We've helped our children learn how to show interest and put others at ease in conversation. Teach them how to be warm and how to be a friend; then they will never be lacking for friends themselves.

✤

How can we adequately describe all that it means to be a mother? As we hear the word "mother," so many images flood our minds and so many feelings fill our hearts: a young mother holding a small infant, a mother cooking in the kitchen, a tired woman surrounded by a mountain of laundry, and bedtime memories so vivid we can almost feel the cool hand caressing our brow and once again hear a voice saying softly, "Good night."

Say the word "mother" and our thoughts may be like a beautiful water-color—soft and peaceful. Say it again and perhaps we see the other side of motherhood—noise, confusion, feelings of exasperation and inadequacy.

Motherhood brings out the best and the worst in all who have joined its ranks. Above all, it is a privilege and a gift given by God. If we do it his way, he will provide all that we need to get the job done right. My deepest desire is that it will one day be said of us:

> Her children rise and call her blessed; her husband also, and he praises her: "Many women do noble things, but you surpass them all." (Proverbs 31:28–29)

Chapter 4

New Mothers

But women will be saved through childbearing—if they continue in faith, love and holiness with propriety.

1 Timothy 2:15

The birth of a child is one of the greatest miracles of life. How utterly amazing it is to look at a tiny newborn who just a short time before was a part of your own body—a little being who had been growing within you for months, who already had brought about so many changes in your life—physically, emotionally and oh, so hormonally!

Now here he or she is, a baby—a real, live human being with two eyes, a nose, a mouth and tiny little fingers and toes. Can anything prepare you for the emotions that run through you as a new parent? They range from utter amazement at the power and creativity of God, to an unfathomable joy and immeasurable sense of love—and then, so often, just a few days later, to another emotion...one of overwhelming panic. You find yourself asking, "What have we done?" and "What do we do now?"

All of our lives have pointed toward this time, yet so many of us finally arrive at motherhood and find ourselves quite unprepared. We are filled with anxieties and insecurities in caring for and raising this seemingly helpless, fragile baby. We live with an exhaustion that cannot be anticipated or described until it has been personally experienced. We have feelings of frustration, confusion and sometimes disappointment.

Even a marriage that has been close and loving and quite compatible suddenly can go through a time of strain and distance. None of us will experience exactly the same difficulties, but believe me, we all will be tested!

Sound pretty discouraging? Although raising children is one of the most challenging and demanding things we will ever do, it is absolutely one of the most fulfilling.

I cannot explain here all that Paul meant when he wrote our theme scripture, 1 Timothy 2:15. Obviously there is much more than what I will apply, but I do believe that bearing and raising children is undeniably one of God's greatest ways of developing and refining our character as women. Rearing children will expose weaknesses that we must conquer and will produce opportunities to mature as nothing else will.

There are so many experiences to be had and adjustments to be made as a new mother. I've been through "the new baby" four times. Honestly, the first time around was the most difficult for me. It was all so different and so unexpected. I simply had no idea how completely my life would change with the arrival of my first child!

The major adjustments that come with motherhood are in the areas of time, marriage and spirituality. You will confront others to be sure, but if you deal with these, you can handle the rest.

Time Adjustment

Every time I had a baby, I was amazed at how one tiny six- or seven-pound baby could put my entire life, and my household as well, into such total chaos! The baby couldn't walk, couldn't talk, mostly ate and slept, and yet if anyone were to innocently ask me, "What did you do all day?" I would have to honestly tell them, "I don't know, but I haven't eaten, haven't gotten dressed, haven't made my bed, and I'm completely and utterly exhausted!" And yet, as out-of-control as things were initially, it was possible to gain some semblance of order in my life...and you can too.

> Be careful, then, how you live—not as unwise but as wise, making the most of every opportunity, because the days are evil. (Ephesians 5:15–16)

Be patient

It gets easier! Six months from now you will step back and smile as you see yourself juggling (and I mean literally "juggling") so many more things in your life with ease. You will learn and you will get better at it.

Be organized and flexible

The reason life is thrown into such confusion after having a baby is that most of us are not used to the constant interruptions that a newborn brings. We've got to learn how to alter our activities when our baby needs us, and yet organize our lives in such a way as to still accomplish other things as well.

We must establish a rhythm and pattern in our lives. God is a God of order and we are made in his image. Just as there is a definite pattern to creation, so we also are made to thrive on order in our lives.

Even babies have a need for routine. Have you ever noticed a child's sense of timing? Babies wake up to be fed at regular intervals. As they get older, children know instinctively when it is time for lunch or their favorite TV program. I have found that the more strong-willed, emotional, and intense the child, the more important it is to provide routine for things like eating, sleeping and bathing. Watch for the signs of his or her natural body-clock, and try to schedule the baby's life, and yours, around it.

Babies and children need a regular bedtime. It should not be different every night. I am convinced that many young children who seem to be completely out of control are actually in desperate need of some predictability in their helpless little lives. If you are putting them to bed whenever you happen to get around to it each night, then you, and they, will pay the price. Establish a routine. You will have calmer, happier children and a much more peaceful home.

On the other hand, children can be amazingly flexible when there is the inevitable change in routine. They won't die if awakened from a nap. They will not automatically become sick because they go to bed late one night. In fact, while I believe very much in the need for routine, I just as fervently believe that all of us must learn to adjust to the unexpected happenings of life.

We helped our young children to become more flexible by putting them down to sleep in other places besides our home. Each one of them had his or her own blanket or comforter which I carried with me. If they needed a nap and we could not be home, I could still put them to sleep with the familiarity of their own blanket.

They also had a special song of their own that I always sang when putting them to bed. Elizabeth loved "Silent Night" and "Now the Day is Over." Jonathan and Alexandra chose "Jesus Loves Me" (each preferred a different verse), and David, for some unknown reason, insisted on "Baa Baa Black Sheep." To each his own! If we were away from home or if someone else had to put them to bed, I or the baby sitter could sing the song and bedtime was essentially the same. In this way, I brought some flexibility into the routine I had established.

Learn to work around the 'good times' and 'fussy times'

Often a young baby is happy and contented in the morning. He or she may take longer naps and require less attention. Use this time to get as much done as possible. This is when you can have your quiet time, take care of the house, and spend time with other people.

If your baby has a particularly difficult time of day (often it will be in the late afternoon), plan your schedule accordingly. Many babies love to ride in the car and will immediately calm down and even go to sleep as soon as the engine starts. This may be when you want to go out and do errands. Or, if your baby enjoys bath time, switch it to this usually unpleasant part of the day. Above all, think. Be creative, be positive and be solution oriented.

When David was a baby he would get irritable in the late afternoon. However, I noticed that he loved the brightness of the tile, lights and chrome in the bathroom. He would get very quiet, almost mesmerized, whenever I took him in there. I often would put him in his infant carrier, place him on the floor in the middle of the bathroom with all the lights on, and run to start dinner. I could usually count on ten to twenty minutes of working before he would start up again.

Be a wise woman—watch for what works, and keep on doing it. Understand that your baby and his schedule will continually change. He will gradually lengthen the time between feedings, and the times spent awake and asleep will be different. The challenge is that as they change, we must also adjust. I remember how difficult it sometimes was when I felt I had finally gotten some control over their schedules and mine, and then they grew and everything changed. The good news is that they also become more predictable. Trust me—it does get easier.

Accept the fact that you probably won't ever feel like everything is finished or done perfectly

This has to be one of the most difficult things for many new parents to accept. Pray that you will do the most important things for that day. Do the very best you can, be thankful for what you did accomplish, and start again tomorrow. Be patient with yourself—as time goes by, you will handle more and more!

Make the most of short periods of time

It takes less than twenty minutes to meet or visit a neighbor, write a card, call a friend or new acquaintance, or fold a basket full of laundry. Learn to exploit the short blocks of time, rather than waiting for the large amounts that never seem to come.

Simplify

Take added pressures off whenever possible. Prepare easy meals. An especially difficult day is not the time for a four-course gourmet dinner. Plan out your menus earlier in the day or by the week. Don't wait until after you have had a baby screaming for two hours to try to come up with a great idea for dinner.

Be hospitable

You can still reach out to other people, but you may need to simplify. When cooking, make two and freeze one. Order pizza occasionally. Can't handle company for dinner? Have them over for dessert and coffee instead.

Operate more from the home

For some of us, home has been more of a rest stop, a place where we go to sleep and freshen up before leaving again. With a new baby, it's not quite so easy to "pick up and go" as before. Titus 2:4-5 says

> Train the younger women to love their husbands and children, to be self-controlled and pure, *to be busy at home*, to be kind, and to be subject to their husbands, so that no one will malign the word of God. (emphasis mine)

Learn not to just *stay home*, but to *be busy at home*. We need to spend more time in our neighborhoods, to have more people into our homes, and let our evangelism be focused where we live. We don't realize how much more is seen, how much brighter our lights shine as Christians, when people can see us as we really are, in our own homes.

Adjust to working or staying at home

Our world has changed dramatically in the past twenty to thirty years. With all of the technological advances, life has become easier and yet busier than ever before. It is more expensive to live and to raise a family. It is also true that most of us are accustomed to nicer things and more of them. This has added a great deal of confusion and pressure to the issues of mothers working. I cannot tell you what you should or should not do. This is a very personal decision, one that you and your husband must make together and for yourselves. There is not a right or a wrong on this, but there is a "what is best" for your family and your situation. I do offer some things to consider that may help you make a wise decision:

1. Know what you are able to handle. The principle I have to live by is "How much can I handle and still act like a Christian?" Some women can handle much more than others and still be gracious, pleasant and godly. Yes, we can and should all grow in our ability to be organized and efficient, but some of you (me included!) are not able to handle the same fast pace as others.

2. What is your financial situation? What kind of debt do you have? What are your fixed expenses? How much income is necessary for you to take care of these? The truth is that many of us must work, if not full time, then at least part time; if not forever, then at least, for the present. In looking at your financial situation, ask this question: while my children are young, is it possible for me to work part time, or is it necessary to work full time?

3. Who will be taking care of my children? You must make sure that your children are in a safe and loving environment, surrounded by the kind of influences you want for their lives. If they are away from you for hours at a time, you must be careful of the things they see and hear. Are they being exposed to things that will hurt their innocence or their confidence?

When Alexandra was just four years old, I enrolled her in a pre-school near our home in New Jersey. I was working in the ministry and thought that she was in a great situation. Academically, it was great, but I did not know until later some of the very harsh and hurtful things that were being said to the children. For some children, those things just rolled off, but for Alexandra they did not. She still remembers those things that were said and how alone and helpless she felt, and I feel guilty every time she speaks of them! I am not saying any of this to put a greater burden on working mothers who may already feel guilty or inadequate, but I am urging you to consider carefully the situations in which you leave your children.

4. If I am working to help us financially, have I considered the costs of childcare, gasoline, and other added expenditures necessitated by my working? Will the money that I can earn be enough to really help, and is that amount worth the time, energy and added pressure to my family?

5. What do I want to do? It is not wrong to consider your own desires. Obviously the decision must be based on more than just your own wants, but they do have a place in this decision. Am I a better, more loving and patient wife and mother because I do something else that I enjoy for a given amount of time each week? Some women really desire to use their talents and their education, and there is nothing wrong with that as long as you can handle the time and the added pressure.

I think the real question you must ask yourself is "Does this allow me to be a better, happier wife and mother, or does it take the best of me away from my family?" My daughter, Elizabeth, is now the mother of three small children. As much as she loves and enjoys being a mother, she has found that she is a better mother when she has some time away each week. She loves writing and several years ago started her own editing business. She has a babysitter who comes several afternoons a week, and she either leaves the house to go and write, or she hides at her desk and works while the children are taken care of. It has been good for her, enjoyable for her children and definitely helpful financially.

6. If you must work, don't fight it; accept it! As far as to work or not to work, I have probably done it all. I stayed at home full time; I worked part time; I taught pre-school and took the children with me; I did some part-time work from home and part-time work away from home; I worked both part time and full time in the ministry; I sold real estate and ran a small clothing business—all of this during the years that I had children at home. I get tired just thinking about it.

I do believe it is best for a mother to be home, as much as possible, with her young children to care for them, to train them and to enjoy a time that goes by all too quickly. If your lifestyle can be adjusted and enough income brought in on one salary, then consider staying home with your young children. If a mother can work part time, allowing her more time at home with her children, that is a good thing.

However, if this is not possible—and there are so many families where it is not—you must not resent and resist something that you cannot change. You will waste valuable time, and you will steal from your family what they need most from you: your love, your joy and your peace. The time you spend fretting over your time away from your children will be better used planning, organizing and doing the work of running a busy schedule and life, and loving your husband and children.

If you cannot change it, then accept it; learn to do it, and do it well. God thinks you can succeed or there would be a way out.

Marriage Adjustment

...and do not forsake your mother's teaching.
They will be a garland to grace your head
and a chain to adorn your neck. (Proverbs 1:8–9)

I thank God every day for allowing me to be raised by the parents he gave me. I have truly been blessed, not only with love and support, but with some incredible examples and teachings that have been indelibly imprinted on my heart. I'm sure as my mother said some things over and over again, she must have wondered if I was really "getting it."

Those things that I did "get" have truly been "garlands to grace my head" and "chains that have adorned my neck." How many times did she say, "Geri, don't be so loud;" "Geri, don't be so bossy" (still a tough one!); "Pretty is as pretty does;" and "God must always be first in your life." These are the teachings I still remember vividly. Some have refined my life; others have become the foundation.

But there was another truth that my mother taught and modeled for all four of her children: "You are a wife first and a mother second. Your children will grow up and leave, but your husband is with you forever." Seeing this put into practice in my home as I grew up, and even more—knowing that this is God's plan—carried us through some of the toughest adjustments of our marriage. Some go through hard times in the year or so after a new marriage, but for many others, the birth of a baby brings the first great challenge to what has been a solid, loving marriage.

In so many marriages, pregnancy and the birth of a first child is the time when love cools and is never rekindled. No one could have prepared me for the new and unexpected intensity of a mother's love for her baby. It is an emotion given by God—but it must be used in a godly way! Yet, so often, in the unexpected intensity of this love, the emotions of warmth, love and even "need" for her husband fades. He can be completely shut out or treated like a hired hand—there for your convenience, to do your bidding. Sounds terrible, but I have seen it over and over again in Christian marriages. It is wrong, it is ungodly, and it will hurt your child's future more than you can know.

Emotions and feelings come and go. They may be great, but they cannot be treated as facts; they must be under the control of what is righteous and true. Decide to believe and act on fact and godly truths, and the right feelings and emotions will follow.

Decide that you will love your husband first and forever.

Decide now that you both are the parents! This is not "your baby," "my baby"...this is "our baby." I've seen so many young mothers consumed with the baby and his or her needs, treating the new young fathers as mere appendages to the family who know nothing and can do nothing right. Nothing could be more destructive to your marriage as well as to the future relationship of respect and admiration your child needs to have for his or her father.

Decide to be close emotionally and sexually. "...and the two will become one flesh" (Matthew 19:5). Decide to be warm and expressive and affectionate, not distant and preoccupied. So many couples who had enjoyed an exciting and fulfilling sexual relationship before pregnancy never seem to get back to that point, much less take it higher after childbirth.

For many women, dealing with the physical satisfaction of nursing and cuddling an infant, not to mention what appears at first, to be irreparable damage to her figure, causes her sexual desires to drop to almost nothing. While that may be what you feel—or should I say, don't feel—you've got to fight to get that part of your marriage back on track. You need to be functioning as "one flesh" as soon as possible after the birth of your baby—usually within four to six weeks.

You may not have yet regained your desire, but you still need the closeness and intimacy that the sexual relationship alone can provide. You need it, and your husband needs it. In due time, a diminished sexual appetite will be awakened by your love and perseverance, but not by waiting for lightning to strike as the two of you drift further and further apart. No, you are not crazy; and no, you are not abnormal. And, be assured, it will not be this way forever—but for now, you may have to work at rekindling the fires of romantic love between you.

Spiritual Adjustment

> Unless the LORD builds the house,
>   its builders labor in vain
> Sons are a heritage from the LORD,
>   children a reward from him. (Psalm 127:1a, 3)

Years ago, I remember reading an article describing something done in the new fathers' waiting room of a hospital. A box was set out, inviting each new father to contribute the thoughts and reactions he experienced during the time of childbirth. As I read the notes reprinted in the magazine, I was moved as, almost without exception, these men talked about their renewed faith in a powerful Creator and a deep sense of reverence and gratitude for God. I couldn't help but wonder what happened to those moments of moving faith and spiritual insight in the weeks and months that followed.

Children are among God's most wonderful and amazing blessings. It is impossible to look upon the miracle of a new baby and not feel a renewed sense of awe and faith in the power of an Almighty Creator. And yet, for so many Christians, the birth of a baby and the beginning of a family marks that time in life of a gradual spiritual decline. This is when they become weak spiritually, more and more consumed with self and the world, never to recover and be as strong and productive as they once were. As a result, God's greatest blessing has become one of Satan's most insidious weapons to kill us spiritually.

You don't have to plummet spiritually now that you are a mother. It doesn't have to happen! God's plan and desire is that childbirth will not destroy us spiritually, but in fact, help us to be saved!

Let me remind you, having a baby is a tremendous adjustment in every way, in every area of your life. You will have to make spiritual adjustments. It will take determination to maintain a deep, meaningful and growing walk with God. Our relationship with God is a relationship of love and commitment and faith. Just as the closeness between husband and wife is tested and must be fought for, so also we must fight to stay close to the Lord.

Don't be surprised at the "spiritual slump" you may find yourself in. But do not allow yourself to stay there! Often the most distressing thing to deal with is a feeling of sluggishness and lack of motivation, as well as a sense of let-down and even depression.

Some women experience this to a greater degree than others.

One young Christian mother described it well as "the baby fog." Understand that much of this is the result of fatigue and hormones that are completely out of balance. Realize it, accept it, but on the other hand, fight and make every effort to "never be lacking in zeal, but keep your spiritual fervor, serving the Lord" (Romans 12:11). Sometimes you just have to do what is right, giving and serving; your emotions and zeal will come back.

James 4:7–8 says,

> Submit yourselves, then, to God. Resist the devil, and he will flee from you. Come near to God and he will come near to you.

Let me give you a few practical suggestions that may help you to prevent or overcome a spiritual slump:

1. Get as much rest as you can in the first few weeks following childbirth. Don't try to be superwoman. Let your body recover and get to know your new baby. But don't become overly preoccupied with yourself, either!

2. Maintain a personal relationship with the Lord whether you feel close to him or not: "in season or out." Try different times for your special time with God until you find what works best: early mornings, after your husband leaves, during your lunch time at work, early afternoon when the children are napping.

Use feeding times to pray and meditate. Be realistic. It is better to consistently spend ten to twenty focused minutes with God every day than to unrealistically try to find an hour that may not be there. Lengthen the time as you can. Above all, be consistent.

3. Take advantage of this special opportunity. Being a new mother will help you reach out to people and share your faith.

Everyone loves babies. People will never be so easy to meet! But, do talk about more than just your baby and yourself!

4. Stay involved with other Christians. Keep in touch with other people by phone, email, and/or time spent together. It's amazing what you can do while cradling a phone to your neck or using Bluetooth. I became adept at nursing a hungry baby, preparing dinner, and mopping up spills with my foot, all while carrying on a somewhat meaningful conversation on the telephone.

5. Come to services and functions of the church.

> Let us not give up meeting together, as some are in the habit of doing, but let us encourage on another—and all the more as you see the Day approaching. (Hebrews 10:25)

Satan is at work trying to sabotage your efforts to grow spiritually. Decide, "I need to be there!" Mothers, your babies are flexible. They can go places. They can miss occasional naps. They can even be left for a time with other reliable people. But it does take planning and some perseverance. You will have to allow more time to get ready than you used to, and remember to leave some extra time for the unexpected (the dirty diaper, the fall, the tantrum or the upset stomach), which will always happen just before you must leave!

When my first three children were small, I had to get up by 5 a.m. on Sunday just so I could arrive by 9:00. I know, I am probably slower than a lot of you, but we lived thirty minutes from the church building and because Sam was either getting ready to preach or had to be there early, I was on my own getting the children up and ready. It was hard but absolutely worth it.

To be honest, I have been deeply disturbed at the lack of commitment to God's church that I see in many young families.

I know it is not easy getting children dressed, fed and ready for church. It is not "fun" bringing children home from church when they are exhausted and have missed their naps or their bedtimes. And it is especially challenging when you have been away at work all day. But, mothers, it is exceedingly worth the effort! You need the teaching of God's word and the fellowship of God's family, and your children need to see that priority in your lives.

I remember how difficult some of those times were, but I also know that my children grew up loving God and his church as a result of those efforts. In fact, while I can still remember some of the struggles, they remember those times as precious memories of childhood. Remember what Jesus said: "But seek first his kingdom and his righteousness, and all these things will be given to you as well" (Matthew 6:33).

6. Get advice from mature, spiritual women. Let them help you decide about sickness—when to take your baby out and when to leave him or her at home. I don't believe in exposing healthy children to sicknesses or in dragging sick children around, but I also know that some young children live with slight sniffles most of their lives, yet are not contagious or really sick. Get help and advice!

Ask other Christians, "Am I doing too much, pushing too hard, could I or should I be doing more?"

Cherish the Time

As I conclude this chapter for new mothers, let me urge you to enjoy your children. Watch everything they do with joy, pride and amazement. You are watching a miracle of God unfold before your very eyes. Appreciate it, enjoy it, and revel in the mystery of it. Ironically, just as we begin to feel confident in handling our infant, he or she turns into...a toddler!

I vividly remember when, on Elizabeth's third birthday, she went up to her father and said, "Daddy, when will I be two again?" I still remember the look Sam and I gave each other as we told her, "Never, honey...you'll never be two again."

Years later, I stand in wonder and awe at the beautiful young woman she has become. What happened to that tiny little girl, the one who kept me up so many nights as a newborn, the two-year-old who challenged my authority (and my confidence) as no one ever had, the four-year-old who, when she didn't get her way, threatened, "I won't be your best friend!"? Yet today, she is indeed my best friend.

What happened to the years? They flew by so quickly. I remember singing to her the song "Sunrise, Sunset" as she sat in her little infant carrier eating her first taste of cereal. Even then, I had a deep sense of how short the time would be. And it was. The years did pass and now, she is a young mother with babes of her own.

Young mothers, cherish this time, laugh at the craziness of it, cry at the shortness, remember all you can, and above all, let these days and weeks and years be the time for God to mold and shape you into all you were meant to be.

Part 2
Fundamentals

Chapter 5

The Four Essentials

> These commandments that I give you today are to be upon your hearts. Impress them on your children. Talk about them when you sit at home and when you walk along the road, when you lie down and when you get up.
>
> Deuteronomy 6:6–7

Whatever else you may learn from this book, learn this chapter! These principles are the basics, the critical essentials. They need to be second-nature in your parenting. The four essentials are: love, respect, obedience and honesty. We will discuss each one thoroughly.

The First Essential: Love

Jesus was asked once which was the most important commandment of all. Of everything that God wants from us, what is at the top of his list? The answer came back, without hesitation, crisp and clear:

> "'Love the Lord your God with all your heart and with all your soul and with all your mind.' This is the first and greatest commandment. And the second is like it: 'Love your neighbor as yourself.' All the law and the Prophets hang on these two commandments." (Matthew 22:37–40)

Love is of first importance. All else is secondary. Peter declares that "above all" we should have love (1 Peter 4:8). Paul says that even if we possess the great qualities of eloquence, prophecy, wisdom, faith, and if we sacrifice to the point of martyrdom, but lack love, we are "nothing" (1 Corinthians 13: 2).

We may lavish upon our children the finest things and the most expensive and stylish clothes; we may take them on the most exciting vacations and send them to the most prestigious schools; but if we do not make them feel loved, it is all to no avail. How many children have all of these things, yet remain empty, angry, depressed and discontented, simply because they do not feel close to their parents?

If there is closeness and love between our kids and us, we have a place to stand and a place to start. They are connected to us. They want to please us. They long to be near us. We have won the greatest battle of all—the battle for their hearts. But if there are no bonds of love, we are relegated to a ceaseless battle of wills in which there can never be a true victor.

As parents then, what we want to have, and what we want to give—above anything else—is love. If we build our families on love, our kids will be strong. Children raised in homes that are saturated with love are far less likely to be drawn into cliques of worldly kids or into lawless gangs. Loving families are bulwarks and fortresses against the temptations, traps and corrosive effects of the world, serving to prevent many problems from ever gaining a foothold.

Kids are born with the capacity to love, but not all learn how. What can we do to get love into our children's lives?

1. Teach Them About God's Love

Jesus loves me! this I know,
for the Bible tells me so;
little ones to him belong;

They are weak but he is strong.
Yes, Jesus loves me;
Yes, Jesus loves me;
Yes, Jesus loves me;
The Bible tells me so.

These immortal words of Anna B. Warner have become the anthem of children all around the world. And so it should be. Little ones should be raised in an atmosphere saturated with God's love. They should be taught from infancy that God cares for them, knows all about them, takes delight in them, and longs to be close to them. Kids must grasp that God is a personal being who will be the closest friend they will ever have. *Your children's view of God is the most important lesson you will ever teach them.* It shapes their whole view of life and reality.

How many of us grew up with a negative view of God—a distant, dismal, impossible-to-please dictator whose frown of disapproval darkened the sunny days of our childhood? Some of us have spent years unlearning the intellectual and emotional view we at one time had of God.

Let's take the opportunity to teach our children from their youngest years about the great God of the Bible, the God who made them, sees them, longs to be their Father, and desires to be with them in heaven forever.

Teach them of the God who is their shepherd, who knows them by name, who watches over them all the time, and who has even assigned them a personal angel (Matthew 18:10). They need to see that God is like Jesus, and that Jesus loved children and always took time to be with them.

2. Love Your Children

Most parents love their children, and you do, too, or you wouldn't be reading this book. What we need to talk about is how we can more *effectively communicate* and *express* our love. Our goal is to not only love our kids, but to help them know how much we do. The more secure our children feel in our love, the easier it will be for us to train, discipline and raise them.

If we are not careful, we can allow our parenting to become focused upon a battle of wills, rather than upon enjoying a loving and nurturing relationship. This is not to say that we will not have our challenges with a child, but it is to say that in the midst of those struggles we can grow in being more affectionate and expressive.

We must take care that the energy we expend and the frustrations we experience do not cause us to become a negative or resentful parent. Life can be overwhelming, and we may find that we have unwittingly become so wearied by our own problems that our children may feel that we treat them as if they were just another of our many burdens to bear.

Let's face it—as kids become older, we may have a harder time getting along with them. We might even have to confess that even though we genuinely love our kids, we sometimes have a hard time *liking* them very much!

Well, don't think you are alone if you wrestle with those feelings from time to time. To love our children, we need to depend upon Jesus and our Father in heaven. They are our examples and sources of love, and they teach us to love as they have loved us.

But how can we love our children?

Love each one

Each of our children should be special to us. We cannot play favorites without suffering the consequences. That was the error of Isaac and Rebekah (Genesis 25:28) and Jacob (Genesis 37:4). The result in their family was catastrophic. Each child should feel they have their own unique place in our hearts. Yes, there will be some kids who are easier to like and easier to be with. But we must imitate God in his absolute, unconditional love.

Love with your time and attention

We should notice our children and be aware of them. Whatever their age, we need to be tuned in to their needs. We cannot be so distracted by life that we become insensitive to their problems. Some children demand attention; others don't seem to need as much. The former must not drive us away or take up all our time, and we cannot neglect the latter.

It just takes time. In many ways, kids look at the time we give them as the most direct expression of our love. If we do not set aside time to be with them exclusively, they will not feel loved. If we find ourselves continually saying, "Not now; I'm busy," then it is time to reexamine our attitude and our priorities. If we do not take the time now, we will try later, but it may be too late.

The love and attention that Jesus gave to children during his busy ministry tells us the kind of priority that we should give to our kids. On the occasion when his disciples sought to block the intrusion of little ones into his presence, Jesus became indignant. He publicly rebuked his misguided followers and stopped what he was doing to spend time with the kids:

> People were bringing little children to Jesus to have him touch them, but the disciples rebuked them. When Jesus saw this, he was indignant. He said to them, "Let the little children come to me, and do not hinder them, for the kingdom of God belongs to such as these." (Mark 10:13–14)

With this example of our Lord before us, as busy as he was, dare any of us say we are too busy for our children? Time can be spent in longer stretches, such as going for a walk, playing or reading, but it can also be spent by taking a moment to pause and give a few precious minutes of total attention. We are wise when we take our children with us as we go out to run errands— we get two things done at once. (Unless we spend the whole time talking on our cell phones!)

Mostly, what they want and need, in any form they can have it, is some exclusive time spent with Mom and Dad. Such time says "I love you" in ways nothing else can.

Love with your touch

> "I tell you the truth, anyone who will not receive the kingdom of God like a little child will never enter it." And he took the children in his arms, put his hands on them and blessed them. (Mark 10:15–16)

I am sure Jesus could have blessed the children from afar; he could have smiled and waved as his limo rolled by. But antiseptic, impersonal "contact" was not his way; his was the way of closeness and affection.

We all need to be touched. There is nothing like the magic of human contact. Touch expresses what words and deeds cannot. God made us to need affection. We dry up emotionally without it. Read through the Gospels and note the number of times Jesus touched or was touched by someone. Touch is the language of love and intimacy. It breaks down barriers and says, "I love you. We are close and connected. You have nothing to fear."

Let's not allow our family to be aloof and distant from one another. All of us have observed households where there is iciness and a reserve that is stifling, stuffy and sour. That's just not much fun for anybody. Children raised in such an atmosphere develop a hard, nasty edge of anger and meanness. They are more prone to be disobedient, obstinate and to feel distant from parents. They are also more likely to have sexual hang-ups and marriage difficulties.

Some of us were raised in unaffectionate families. Perhaps there was love, but it was rarely expressed in direct or outward form. If so, we must realize that God has a better plan for us now. Throughout the Scriptures, physical affection is modeled and enjoined: The father and son embraced and kissed in the parable of the prodigal son (Luke 15:20). God commands us to greet one another in the church with a holy kiss (Romans 16:16, 1 Corinthians 16:20). Paul and the church leaders in Ephesus embraced and kissed (Acts 20:37). God wants there to be generous expression of affection in his family, the church, and in our homes as well.

I remember going away to college and visiting a church where there was lots of warmth and hugging. I was not from a background where physical affection was very prominent. It blew my mind! I at first thought that there must be something wrong with these people. But as I continued to attend, I realized that I was the one with the limited view of love. I began to change, and it produced a wonderful transformation in all my relationships, especially with those closest to me.

I touch and embrace my wife and children frequently. I found that as my kids grew past infancy and the toddler years that they still needed hugs, pats on the back, kisses on the cheek—actions that clearly said, "I love you."

If we as parents feel inadequate in this area, we can learn a better way. We can grow, and we can break down our pride, our inhibitions, our fears, our starchiness, and give our kids the love they crave. Strive to be more affectionate at home—your love will be the oil in the hard machinery of life.

Love with your expressions

By this I mean our facial expressions, our smiles, the look in our eyes, and our tone of voice. Children notice and read these things like a book. Harsh words and surly frowns do not give our kids a good feeling. Smile often at your children. This may seem like an obvious thing but note this week—how often do you look your child in the eyes and smile approvingly?

My wife, Geri, has an amazing way of expressing love with her joyful voice, warm smile and sparkling eyes. When we are conversing with others, she is so engaging that I can barely get anyone to look my way. I have often found myself leaning my head at some ridiculous angle towards my wife so I will be noticed!

I finally figured out that it wasn't because Geri is so beautiful (which she most certainly is) or because I am so ugly (no comment), but because of the smiling attentiveness she gives. Her voice is almost musical with a positive "up" tone about it. She laughs frequently—even at my lousy jokes. Her aura of warmth, joy and cheerfulness brightens and energizes our house and makes even difficult days more pleasant. When this is the atmosphere in our home, kids feel loved, and they love being in our family.

Love with your words

When David was about two years old, he began to come up to me and say, "I love you too, Daddy!" I appreciated this, but it puzzled me. Was senility already upon me, in my early thirties? Was I going around saying "I love you" to my son and not remembering five seconds later?

I then realized that David had learned to say he loved me because of all the times he had heard me say it to him first. Therefore, his way of expressing it always came out as a response.

Do we get the point? Saying the words "I love you" to our kids teaches them to love. They are born as a blank slate. They have the capacity to love but must be taught how by being shown and by being told they are loved.

We just can't overdo it here. Kids need to hear the words "I love you" spoken sincerely and frequently by both parents. We also need to tell them what it is we love and like about them and what makes them special. Express love at important times like bedtime, leaving for and returning from school—and anytime you sense a hurt or fear. Of what are the precious memories of childhood made? Not the expensive things and experiences we provide, but from the "little moments" of being happy and close.

3. Teach them to love others

As they have been loved, so they should love. Kids who are showered with love must be taught to give it away. If we do not teach our children to love, they will become selfish, aloof and arrogant. God loves us, but he commands us to love him in return and to love others as we love ourselves.

Parents, we must imitate God's fatherly love in the way we expect our children to love us, love their siblings, and love those outside the family. Love is more than a natural response to being loved; it is a deliberate decision a child makes in response to the teaching and expectations of parents.

Love and concern for others should be talked about consistently, encouraged and praised. Teach them expressions of love and to respond when people speak to them. It is rude when children ignore or shrug away the greetings of others. Teach them to look at people when they speak.

Children also learn to love by helping. They are capable of so much more than we think. Sometimes it seems the most conscientious and caring parents have the lowest expectations for their children. We slavishly serve them, expect little from them, and in so doing raise our kids to be self-centered.

The family is a great place to teach our children to be sensitive, serving and cooperative. It is the workshop in which we teach the older to watch out for the younger, and the younger to respect the older.

We worked long and hard on this one. We had "servant's week" when everyone tried to "outdo one another in service." We gave out stickers and made up charts to establish happy, helpful habits. We emphasized that the way we treat one another is actually the way we are treating Jesus himself (Matthew 25:34-40).

Children must come to understand that the whole family is an instrument of God to serve and reach out to others. Loving, obedient children of Christian parents are one of the brightest lights that God can use to illuminate a dark world. Encourage your kids to invite friends, teachers and acquaintances to church and to pray for specific people to come to know the Lord. Let them experience the power of God at work through their lives and their prayers. They can learn very early to be "people lovers" with the great purpose of helping the poor and needy, and helping others learn about Christ.

Our oldest son, David, was shy and withdrawn in his early years. He seemed not to need people and could drift away into his own little world. Geri and I decided that this behavior needed to change and that we would do our best to teach David to be friendly, to care about and to connect with others. We started encouraging him to look at people's faces when they spoke to him, smile and say, "Hi."

Among family and close friends we gave him lots of affection and taught him to become more warm and expressive. We shared repeatedly with him biblical principles like "freely you have received, freely give" and "give and it shall be given to you." All of this was done positively, firmly and consistently without making him feel self-conscious. We firmly believed he could be, in his own special way, a giving, warm, friendly child.

The results were very encouraging. Over time, David grew to be an outgoing, confident young man who related easily with people. His retained his sensitivity, but learned to direct it toward the feelings and concerns of others and not just toward himself.

David could have grown up as a socially withdrawn introvert who lived far beneath his potential. Instead, because of being shown love and being taught how to love others, he matured to become a giving, confident young man.

The Second Essential: Respect

"Honor your father and mother"—which is the first commandment with a promise—"that it may go well with you and that you may enjoy long life on the earth." (Ephesians 6:2–3)

The issue of respect for authority in the lives of children is absolutely critical. I am appalled at the arrogant, haughty, cocky attitudes I see in some children. They do not respect God, their parents, their teachers, adults, their babysitters or other children. This is a devastating trend in our society, and we must confront it in our churches as well. If we do not address and overcome this problem when we see it in our churches and homes, we will suffer a frightful loss of our kids to the world.

Many of us are blind to the fact that our children are arrogant and disrespectful. I am shocked at the attitudes and behaviors that many parents allow to go unchecked in their children. And I am not just talking about people out in the world; I am talking about Christians—disciples who ought to know better.

Maybe we think it's cute, or maybe we think this is the way all children are. I am afraid that some of us, in an attempt to make our kids into confident, strong, leader-types, have bred into our children an attitude of superiority, conceit and cockiness. We will live to reap the bitter harvest of our folly.

Pride is not a necessary accompaniment of confidence. Pride is repugnant and offensive to God at any level, at any age, and must be dealt with firmly.[1]

How can we tell if our children are disrespectful? In younger children, it will come out with sassy talk, defiant looks, temper tantrums, stomping feet and hitting at you. With older kids it can be all the above, plus slamming doors, rolling eyes and muttering. The list is endless, and I'm sure many of us can add more to it.

Our position of honor and authority as parents is given to us by God. Our authority does not come because we are perfect; it is because God in his wisdom has so arranged it. For our children to honor us is to show honor to God and his plan. As our children come to respect our authority, they learn to respect God himself; and then one day, when they are old enough, they will give God the ultimate honor of committing their lives to him. Therefore, parents, claim your authority. Expect to be respected. If you do not expect it, you will not get it.

Sometimes, we as parents lack confidence in dealing with kids. We feel guilty and inadequate. We become tentative. We suggest, plead, argue, wheedle and cajole. Our children sense our self-doubt, and they become more defiant. They also become less secure because what they really want down inside is the confidence that comes from knowing their limits.

They want us to put a fence around them—a fence that tells them just how far they can go. We need to put up the fence and tell the kids exactly where it is. They will try to run through it to see if it is real. Let them hit it a few times. They will soon learn that the fence is immovable but that within it they have total freedom and security. Then you will have respect.

---

1. These words were written in 1994. Indeed, in the years following, many churches experienced an alarming loss of young people to the world. While there is no single reason for this, it is our observation that a generational absence of respect and reverence for God played a major role in what transpired in those years.

The Third Essential: Obedience

Obedience to parents is the next of the four major areas of training that will produce godly character in our children. Obedience must be taught and expected early. It lays the foundation for obedience to all other authorities in life and ultimately to God.

Children who are rebellious, defiant and disobedient to parents later will demonstrate those same attitudes and behaviors toward all other authorities, be they teachers, babysitters, grandparents, employers, church leaders or law enforcement personnel. Ultimately, they will come to disobey God.

By the time children are eighteen months old, they usually are able to understand most of what is said to them, even though they cannot verbally communicate well. This is when early training of "Come here" and "Don't touch that!" begins. These are not games where they tease us by running away or touching whatever has been set off limits. When we give commands to our children, we speak as the God-ordained adult authority in their lives, and we must patiently, yet firmly expect obedience.

It is much easier to teach children to obey while they are young than to begin years later when the habit of disobedience is deeply established. Some of us have personally experienced the pain and devastation of living uncontrolled, disobedient lives. Let's spare our children the lessons we had to learn the hard way, and teach them obedience while they are young.

Obedience is such a vital area that we will devote our next chapter entirely to this subject.

The Fourth Essential: Honesty

"You will know the truth, and the truth will set you free."
(John 8:32)

> They perish because they refused to love the truth and be
> saved. (2 Thessalonians 2:10)

In order to have a relationship with God, we must love the truth, accept the truth, live by the truth and tell the truth. Acceptance of the truth—for the love of truth alone—is the first and most important building block of character. Telling the truth to ourselves and to others enables us to be free and to have genuine relationships.

Parents, we must teach our children to accept, love and tell the truth. If they learn to accept the truth as children, they will be able to face their sins, repent of them, and be saved when they are older. If they always tell us the truth, no matter how difficult it may be to do so, we are helping them build a life based on righteousness.

Satan is a liar and the father of lies (John 8:44). When our children lie, we must realize they are taking a fateful step that can eventually wreck their lives. We must have deep convictions about this, or we will dismiss our children's deceit as a childish immaturity rather than treat it as a serious character issue. (I am speaking here of deliberate deceit and not harmless childish imagination.) We must catch it the first time it happens, and deal with it swiftly and powerfully.

If we do this, we will not be continually fighting a battle to get our children to tell the truth. We won't have to wonder if we have the whole story. If we do not trust our kids' word, we have a serious problem that we must solve at all costs.

We confronted the lying issue with each of our children at age three. I don't know why, but that's just when each of them told their first lie.

One day, some college students were over at our house. We were outside in the front yard when one of them walked over to me and said, "Elizabeth is coloring all over the front steps. I asked her about it, and she said you gave her permission to do it." I went over, took a look, and sure enough, Elizabeth was coloring away literally *on* the steps.

I said, "Elizabeth, what are you doing?" She looked at me, then at the student, and dissolved into a pool of tears. I knelt down, looked her in the eyes, and said, "Did you lie and say I gave you permission to do this?"

She wailed "Yesssssss!"

I told her that coloring on the steps was bad, but lying was even worse. She could tell by my reaction that this was very serious. I don't remember all the disciplinary action we took, but it was strong. She took it all very much to heart, and learned an important lesson.

With our son David, it was a bit different. He, at age three, began to "not remember" when we would ask him things. To some degree, he was right. David was (and is) so intense that he didn't hear anything unless we had a radar-lock on his eyeballs. But we began to notice increasing incidences of "I don't remember" or "I'm not sure" excuses when he got into trouble. It all came to a head one evening with the famous "Magic Pillows" caper.

David was playing in the family room. He had pulled all the pillows off the couch and onto the floor. I went in and told him that Mom did not want the pillows on the floor, so we put them back up on the couch. David stayed in the family room, and I got busy elsewhere around the house. Within a few minutes I had to go back into the now-empty family room, and I saw the pillows on the floor.

I called David in and asked him if he did the deed. He got a panicky, puzzled look on his face and said, "I can't remember; I don't know." I checked with everyone else in the house and learned that no one else had even been in the room during those few minutes. David had to have been the one who did it since he was the only person who had even been in the room.

But he still could not remember!

It was part fear, part not paying attention to his actions, part mental block, and part self-protection; but I felt it was time for David's memory to function normally. I knew I could not back off; it was time to bring it to a head. David got into such a state of mental lockup that I think he did have trouble remembering whether he did or not.

I explained to him he was the only one who could have done it, unless the pillows were "magic pillows" that in Disney-esque fashion could bounce themselves off the couch! I decided he could not eat with the family until he "remembered." He needed time to think. He had to go to his room and search his memory banks.

It was a lesson he had to learn, or he could conveniently forget anything he wanted, anytime it served his purpose. It took a little while, but finally, David came and told me, "Dad, I think I do remember pulling those pillows off the couch. I am sorry." It was genuine. He had tried with all his might and got himself as far as he could.

I accepted his apology. David's memory has improved remarkably since then! He has learned to be honest with himself, to face the truth, and to not give in to freezing up in panic when he is confronted with something unpleasant.

I tell these stories not to embarrass my children, but to illustrate the importance of taking a stand for truthfulness and to show the different ways children can skirt the truth.

Accepting, living by, and telling the truth are qualities of character that you must model, teach and unflinchingly expect from your young ones. There are other forms of dishonesty that you may face in raising a child. Don't be naive; learn to spot them. Deal with the problem in terms they understand, and you will find you can build honesty into your child's innermost character. Consider these words from Proverbs 12:19:

Truthful lips endure forever,
   but a lying tongue lasts only a moment.

You will probably find that you will need to go back over this chapter time and again. Above all, study the scriptures that are referenced, and along with your spouse come to your own convictions about what you need to do. Patiently and lovingly work to build the kind of foundation your family can stand on for a lifetime. If you depend on God and do not give up, you will see your children blessed as you build your family with love, obedience, respect and honesty.

Chapter 6

Winning Obedience from Children

Discipline your son, and he will give you peace;
he will bring delight to your soul.

Proverbs 29:17

We now come to the nuts and bolts of the real life raising of children. How can we obtain quick and cheerful obedience? How can we train in those qualities of character and habits of conduct that will cause our children to grow up to be a joy to us?

From the very beginning, children should learn to obey. Our intent is to make obedience a pattern, and not a daily battle we fight that makes our lives and theirs miserable. When obedience is a habit, our families are happy. The arguing, yelling and tension that most people consider a necessary evil simply will not exist in our homes. When as parents we exercise the authority that God calls us to have, we will have order, and not chaos. But we must believe that it should be and can be this way, or we will never see it happen.

The first principle of obedience we taught in our home was "first-time obedience." The kids knew that they were to do what they

110

were told immediately. We did not expect to have to tell them over and over again. Children learn quite early just how far they can push us (or any authority) until action will be taken.

Parents, we fall into a terrible trap when we find ourselves repeating our requests over and over, in a louder, more urgent tone, until our words are finally heeded. This is not true obedience. It sets a tone of nagging and arguing that ruins the atmosphere of a home. If this continues, we will find ourselves becoming increasingly weary and frustrated. We can even begin to dislike and resent our kids.

We established this principle of first-time obedience not only by our expectation, but by teaching it in family devotionals and by reinforcing it in passing conversations. We used fun ways of reminding everyone when we found ourselves slipping out of the habit: "When do we obey?" Mom or Dad would ask. "The first time!" replied the kids.

I realize that this principle may sound idealistic, unreasonable or even impossible to some of you. I had one parent express to me that he had found it impossible to implement first-time obedience with his rambunctious three-year-old son, and he went on to note that even God expected that we, his children, would sometimes disobey.

Granted, none of us should be so deluded as to think we will always attain instant obedience from our children, and neither will we always obey our Father in heaven as quickly as we should. But what we want to impress upon you is this: *you get what you expect.* If you expect your children to ignore you, they will. If you expect to have to threaten, beg and cajole them, then that is what you will end up doing. Unless you expect it, quick obedience will be a rarity, at best. But, the good news is that if you expect prompt and respectful obedience, your kids will give it.

Tell me this, when would you prefer your kids to obey? The fourth time? The third? The tenth? Or, would you prefer the

111

first? We all know the answer. Let's start expecting prompt obedience, and let's have some faith in our kids (and in God's word) that they indeed are capable of doing better—much better than what we may be used to—or what we have seen in other families.

If you have a long-standing history of permissiveness, understand that it will take determination, faith and patience to change the pattern. And the older the kids, the more effort it will take. As you assert your will, things may even seem to get worse before they get better. It will take both parents coming to a firm conviction that this is indeed possible and the right thing to do. But, rest assured, the change is well worth the effort! Once the pattern of obedience is in place you will be amazed that the family seems so much happier, relaxed and refreshed.

I had an experience in coaching soccer that brought this principle home to me. We had a nine-year-old named Javier (not his real name) on our team who constantly fought and argued with his parents. He would whine, cry, scream and yell at them in just about every interaction we ever observed both before and after practice. And they answered in kind.

He tried this once with me, and I said to him with a smile on my face and steel in my soul, "Javier, if you want to play soccer on this team, we expect you to do what we ask without fussing and arguing."

He looked at me for a moment, and complied. We never had a problem with him again. He always had a great attitude. His father at the end of the season came to me and said, "Coach, how do you get Javier to cooperate? He is so pleasant and obedient out here, but not with us."

I said, "Roberto, we never for a moment considered that he would *not* do what we asked." His father looked at me as if I was speaking Swahili. He just did not believe things with his son could be different—and that was the problem.

Our second principle of obedience is "parents never lose." Geri and I decided early on that we would not and could not lose any battle of obedience with our children if we were going to be effective parents. If you are ever defeated one time by a child they will be encouraged to challenge you again and again. We had to change our minds on some expectations when we realized we were being unreasonable or were mistaken, but we informed the kids of this at the time so as not to confuse them. We apologized when we felt it was warranted. But we have never just given up or given in, thus losing a battle of wills.

Sometimes the whole issue with a child comes down to one turning point, the epic "mother of all battles" upon whose outcome your future hangs. Such a struggle took place in our family with our son David when he was about two.

We were headed to my mother's home for a visit, about a two-and-a-half hour drive. David was strapped safely in the rear of the car in his car seat. He was well-fed, freshly changed and had plenty of toys with which to play—all set for a nice ride.

He didn't see it that way. He wanted to come up front and sit in his mom's lap. He started crying. Geri checked him again carefully to see if he was comfortable. He checked out fine. He just didn't like his seating assignment.

He got louder. We tried to get him quiet—we sang songs, gave him toys, offered food, all to no avail. It was clear that this young man would be satisfied by one thing and one thing only—to come up front and sit on his mother's lap.

The way I viewed it, there were two good reasons for taking a stand: (1) It would be unsafe for him to travel that way (I am dating myself, but this was before there were car seat laws), and (2) it now had become a matter of principle.

We stopped looking back and drove on. David cried for almost two hours. It was not a fun trip. He finally fell asleep, exhausted, about twenty minutes away from my mother's house. We had won.

Someone might ask, "Why didn't you just have his mother sit in the back with him?" My answer: to do so would have been a compromise that would have led to more compromises, and that would have changed the way our family traveled.

Someone else might say, "Why didn't you spank him and have done with it?"

My answer: I saw that this was a battle of wills that would have to be fought sooner or later and that we needed to exhaust his willpower rather than punish him.

In retrospect, it proved to be the right approach. We never again fought a single battle with David over his being put in the car seat, and he learned that he could not wear us down.

Compromise is one of the most devastating mistakes parents can make, and far too many people make it. It is as if our words mean nothing. We tell our kids to do something and they argue or ignore us. We accept this pattern as "normal," But it is normal only because we let it be.

When we do this, we sow the seeds of rebellion and exasperation (Ephesians 6:4) into our children's hearts by our weakness. They will grow up to experience the infinitely harder disciplines of life, the law and God himself if we do not turn this around.

If you have been failing here, sit down with your children and let them know there are going to be some changes. Get out the Bible, and read them the passages about obeying. Show them about how God has given you the responsibility to raise them and how they have the responsibility to obey.

Talk to them about obeying "the first time." Explain to them that although it has not been that way, that you, and they, are going to change. As best you can, help them to understand what you are doing, why, and that your family will be happier and more pleasing to God as a result.

Have a prayer together, and from that time on, be different. Don't give up until the habit of obedience is permanently established in your home.

Recognizing Disobedience

Half the battle is recognizing when our kids are disobedient. Let's look at four different types of disobedient behavior.

Defiant disobedience

This is fairly easy to spot, even for the wimpiest, most deluded parent. It starts out with "No!" and is often accompanied by a stomping foot and a curled lip. We are shocked and intimidated by such brashness and either give in quickly or wear down over time. Sometimes we debate with them (have you ever found yourself down on the floor arguing with a three-year-old?), or we excuse it by saying, "Well, you're just tired."

The fact, plain and simple, is that you have been beaten. You lack willpower. You are a fearful parent, and you will pay for your compromising ways by raising an insecure, defiant, spoiled brat.

Our oldest daughter, Elizabeth, grew up to be a confident, assertive, respectful young woman. But in her early years, she was incredibly strong-willed and defiant. Things got so bad that on one occasion I found myself searching the Yellow Pages, looking in vain for "Exorcist: We make house calls."

Elizabeth took on Geri and decided she would make a run at being "Head Woman" in our house. Often, I would come home and hear Elizabeth's cries from behind her closed door, and find Geri muttering repeatedly, "I'm going to win, I'm going to win." And win she did!

To do this, it took both of us resolving that we would be lovingly firm and that we could never let her wear us down. At around five years, Elizabeth settled down and became a delight, but that was because she knew she could never defeat us, and that it was in her best interest to obey.

We are convinced that if we had allowed her to conquer us in her early years, she would not have become who she is today

(And Elizabeth, now a grown woman and the mother of her own strong-willed little girl, agrees!)

Disarming disobedience

Have you ever had a kid who could crack you up laughing while he or she was disobeying you? This little manipulator can smile at us, do something funny and melt us right on the spot. We try to justify ourselves by repeating those fateful words: "But aren't you cute!" But the fact is, we lost!

If we let a child control us now by smiling and laughing, we will cry and mourn later. We are creating a child who will learn to charm his or her way through life, manipulating others for personal gain.

Our son Jonathan is a card. He has a dry sense of humor that gets everyone laughing. He does imitations, tells jokes, the whole bit. He began to wear glasses early on, and with the overalls and suspenders that he wore, he looked like a cute, innocent "little professor."

As he got older, and the kids would be cleaning up after dinner, he would do his voices and make jokes while David and Elizabeth dutifully did the work. Then, in the middle of his act, they would suddenly realize what was going on. "Jonathan, you haven't done a thing!" But, too late, the dishes were done!

We learned to enjoy Jonathan, and to laugh with him and at him, but we also had to teach him to learn to work and do his part. We are happy to say that he did indeed learn how to work hard (but he still cracks everybody up in the meantime!).

Deaf disobedience

Some kids act as if we, their parents, don't exist. Our words have no impact on them. We tell them to do something, and we get back silence or an unintelligible grunt, but no action. We

116

repeat our request, but still there is no response. We might even get verbal agreement, but nothing ever happens. This, too, is disobedience—it is passive, and it may go undetected, but it is a serious issue.

Unless you change this pattern it will continue. Your kids will be lazy and slow to obey. They also will learn that you eventually will give up, forget about it, or do it yourself. If you allow this pattern to go unchecked, it ultimately will destroy a child's character, and it will wear you out as well.

Our son David was so adept at deaf disobedience that we had his ears checked for bad hearing. We did this several times, and he tested out fine. I finally came to suspect it was a problem of attitude, not one of hearing. I conducted my own experiment to check out my theory. One afternoon when David was out riding his Big Wheel, I called him in for dinner. It seemed as if he did not hear me, so I called louder. No response. I walked to the curb and called again—not even a flicker of response. Finally, I jumped in his path, grabbed the steering wheel, leaned down and said again, "David, come to dinner NOW!" That's what it took to get his attention.

The next day, I ran another test—similar weather conditions, same Big Wheel, same time of day. Standing at a great distance from where David was riding in the road, I said in hushed tones to Geri, "Why don't we take the kids to get ice cream?"

VROOM! Dust swirled; rocks flew. The smoking tires of the Big Wheel rumbled to a stop dangerously close to my toes. David, his eyes glittering with expectation, looked up at me and said, "Ice cream? Are we going to get ice cream?" I knew from that moment on, David could hear just fine; he had been hearing only what he wanted to hear. We worked with him, taught him to listen, and things improved greatly.

If you have a child who is not listening to you, you must realize how serious it is. I would suggest that you study the Book of Proverbs to deepen your own convictions. Then, sit down, and study those same verses with your children and teach them to give you their attentive, respectful obedience.[1]

Dreary disobedience

This may be the most exasperating and effective resistance to your authority that a child can display. It is utilized by all children to some degree and by some children with deadly effect. I am talking about the tearful, self-pitying, poor-me act that can drive parents into fits of guilt, rage and frustration. This child does not absolutely refuse to obey, but puts up a barrage of moaning and complaining. We either come to believe we are the meanest slave-driver parents who ever lived, or we tire of their whining and give in.

We fail to recognize this behavior for what it is—a serious form of disobedience. We may write it off as "kids being kids" because it seems that all kids do it. We settle for grudging conformity to our wishes, even though it is accompanied by incessant whining and even resentment. To do so is to accept actions done with the wrong attitudes. You must realize that this attitude will one day produce an unhappy, self-pitying adult.

God condemns grumbling and complaining in the Scriptures:

> Do everything without complaining or arguing, so that you may become blameless and pure, children of God without fault in a crooked and depraved generation, in which you shine like stars in the universe as you hold out the word of life. (Philippians 2:14-16)

God does not accept grumbling, resentful obedience from his children. He wants a cheerful, loving acceptance of his will

---

1. Jesus said a great deal about careful listening and its connection with obedience. Cf. Matt. 11:15; 13:1, 13-17, 43; Mk. 4:24. The parable of the soils (Mk. 4:1-23) is a great passage to use to teach kids about listening, hearing and obeying. See also Matt. 7:24-27.

even when it is difficult. If this is what God expects of us, then it is also what we should expect of our children.

In our society, grumbling is pervasive. Whining is a national pastime. We accept it as a fact of life. Even though it makes life unpleasant, and even though the Lord forbids it, we put up with it. I am reminded of another group of spoiled children who grumbled—the children of Israel:

> The rabble with them began to crave other food, and again the Israelites started wailing and said, "If only we had meat to eat! We remember the food we ate in Egypt at no cost— also the cucumbers, melons, leeks, onions and garlic. But now we have lost our appetite; we never see anything but this manna!" ...Moses heard the people of every family wailing, each at the entrance to his tent. The LORD became exceedingly angry, and Moses was troubled. (Numbers 11:4-6, 10)

We learn from other passages that our grumbling when we are inconvenienced might just be grumbling against God. Moses pointed this out when he said, "Who are we? You are not grumbling against us, but the Lord" (Exodus 16:8b). God met the needs of the Israelites when they complained, but he also punished them for their attitude (Numbers 11:33).

As parents we must see that a fussing, whining spirit is offensive to God. It springs from selfishness and ingratitude. God wanted to know the needs of his children, and he did not mind them making their needs known. What he did not accept, and what we must not accept, is complaining. We must teach our kids to be grateful for what they have and not to feel that we and the rest of the world are there to cater to their every pleasure and preference.

Yes, they are young and immature, and we can't expect of kids what we expect of mature adults. But, we need to add ten years onto their age and ask ourselves if we want these attitudes to go unchecked. If we don't start teaching now, our kids may grow into whining, complaining adults.

Some of us grew up in homes where we could not express our feelings and opinions. That is unhealthy and exasperating to children. We don't need to force our kids into sullen silence, but we do need to teach them to express themselves in the right way, at the right time and with the right attitude. Our goal is to cultivate an atmosphere of openness of expression in our home that precludes whining and complaining. We can teach our kids to express their wishes, opinions, likes and dislikes, but in a pleasant, positive tone of voice.

In our family of six there had to be plenty of give and take on things like mealtime menus, seat occupancy, recreational decisions and the like. We taught the kids how to express their wishes and present their point of view without whining and to accept the final decision with a positive attitude. We taught them to say it again with the proper voice tone until it came out right. It will take determination but the establishment of a positive spirit in children is well worth the effort.

The Power of Discipline

What are we to do when our children disobey us? How do we react? What options are open to us? In what follows we provide seven suggestions. Realize that what works in one situation may not work in another and that what is effective with one child may not be effective with another. Use wisdom and trial and error to help you discover what gets the best results.

Verbal correction or reprimand

This is the simplest and most common of all corrective disciplines. It involves the most basic of instructions: "Come here." "Not that way; this way." "Don't do that." "Don't say that."

One-warning rule

If your instructions are not followed, give one verbal warning. If you still are not heeded, then more serious consequences ensue. This principle should be taught to your children, clearly explained to them, and continually reinforced. Once laid out, it should be adhered to consistently.

Immediate correction

The closer to the time of the offense, the more effective the action. If you wait too long, kids have time to forget, distort or rationalize. Delay also creates a tense, fearful atmosphere.

Temporary isolation

This works great with kids who love to be in the middle of the action. Putting them in a corner, into a neutral (boring) room or into their own room can be extremely effective. It prevents them from ruining everyone else's fun with their disobedience. Never let a grumbling, complaining child bring down the whole family's mood. This is actually one way they learn to gain control over us—we simply don't want the disruption, so we let them have their way.

Don't give in. Outsmart them by sending them away with the words, "We're all going to be having a great time out here, and when you get a happy attitude you can come out and join the fun!"

They fret and fuss all alone until they conclude, "No one out there seems to be mourning the loss of my wonderful presence. As a matter of fact, everybody but me is having a blast. I guess I better get my attitude right." But remember, they do not come out until there has been a complete change of heart.

Temporary loss of possessions or privileges

Another way to stay one step ahead of your kids is to deprive them of a special possession or privilege. We have found this to be especially effective if it is reserved for the more serious offenses. It can work with any age and becomes more effective as children grow older. Consider what they love to do or enjoy playing with. Take some time, talk about it with your spouse, and come up with a deprivation of activity or possessions that will help them deal with their misdeeds.

As a youngster of two, David loved his Big Wheel. I don't remember what the horrible crime was, but we said, "You can't ride your Big Wheel for two days." We soon found him sitting stationary upon it, experiencing a voyeuristic fulfillment in spite of our punishment. We said, "You can't even sit on it."

Then we found him standing next to it with a hand on the steering wheel, once again getting a "Big Wheel fix." We went one more step: "David, you can't even touch it." That did it! Now he felt the loss. He stood there in the garage with a faraway look in his eyes, remembering days of glory on his Big Wheel and vowing to never again repeat his crime. It worked so well that this was the only time in his young life that we ever had to take this drastic measure.

Elizabeth, at age three, committed a major offense. "No cookies, Sweetheart, for two days."

"But what about juice and cookies time at preschool?" she protested.

"No, not even there. We will talk to your teachers. You can have the celery and carrots (yum!), but no cookies."

It proved to be very effective. For two days she had to remember and see a consequence for her actions. In this case, it worked better than anything else we could have done.

You will find that this type of action, wisely and judiciously taken, is more effective as children move into the middle school and teen years. Parties, sports leagues, cell phone, video games, iPod, MP3 player, computer privileges, special trips—all these are privileges that can be taken away temporarily to teach a lesson or reinforce an attitude.

The most important aspect of this is to think through it clearly and get help from your spouse before you render judgment. This discipline should be used wisely and be reserved for serious issues. Don't take things away for every offense—this diminishes impact and creates exasperation.

Don't quickly react in anger. How many of us, in the heat of battle, have dictated some foolish punishment, such as, "You are grounded for six months!" only to realize later that the punishment was overkill, unenforceable, or would end up hurting the whole family?

Extra work or jobs to do

Some kids don't mind correction or spankings as long as they got to do whatever they did. To counter this, give extra work. If it relates to the disobedience in some way, it is even more effective. The punishment is actually a form of restitution. Cleaning up the mess they made, taking an extra turn on the dishes, washing the car, working to pay off something purposely or carelessly broken—all of these create a deeper sense of responsibility.

Spanking

What does the Bible say? Is it right or wrong? Consider these verses:

> He who spares the rod hates his son,
>   but he who loves him is careful to discipline him.
> (Proverbs 13:24)

> Folly is bound up in the heart of a child,
>   but the rod of discipline will drive it far from him.
> (Proverbs 22:15)

> Do not withhold discipline from a child;
>   if you punish him with the rod, he will not die.
> Punish him with the rod
>   and save his soul from death. (Proverbs 23:13-14)

The message is clear: Spanking is a valid, recommended and healthy form of discipline. When employed with wisdom and love, it works powerfully. It is virtually irreplaceable in the early years.

Since spanking can be abused and because there is so much legitimate concern today about inappropriate physical punishment, let me give some guidelines on this widely misunderstood subject.

1. A spanking should be an event. We should draw children aside to a private location before spanking them. A spanking is not a "pop" or "whop" out of the blue as we pass by a child we see doing something wrong. Such actions on our part are not only ineffective, but wrong.

2. Explain beforehand the reason for the spanking. Grabbing a child, paddling them, and trying to explain in the midst of the punishment, or afterwards, does no good and is unfair. Not explaining at all is even worse. How can spanking, or any discipline, be effective when the reasons are unstated or unclear? A child should understand the exact reason for the spanking before it is given.

3. Cool off before spanking a child. When we are overly emotional or in a rage, we must wait until we have complete self

control before administering a spanking. When our passions are aroused, we can do and say things that are absolutely wrong. A spanking is a righteous and just discipline, not a retaliatory, frustrated outburst. Screaming, cursing or terrorizing a child is sinful.

4. Use a designated paddle or some flat object as the "rod." The "rod" gives the whole event a judicial air rather than a feeling of personal attack. It is best to decide in advance what to use, so that we don't grab some unsafe implement in the heat of the moment. There are different schools of thought on the definition of the term "rod." Some people believe that it must be a flexible "switch;" others feel the term is not so specific. (Geri and I used a small, flat paddle.) The primary issue is that whatever you use must be weighty enough to get the job done and light enough to inflict no damage or injury.

We should not use our hand to spank with the possible exception of the light slap on the wrist or thigh given to the very young children in the earliest days of discipline. The hand is ineffective with older children and is too personal.

5. Spank on the "safe" backside or thigh. Spankings delivered to these places sting, but do not injure. A spanking should be firm enough to bring tears, but not so hard as to cause bruises or welts. Never strike a child on the face—this is dangerous and degrading. Never strike them on any part of the body where they could be injured. Never should we strike a child with our fists or kick them, push them, slam them into a wall, or throw them to the ground. This is abuse, not discipline. Jerking a child around by the hand or arm is disrespectful and dangerous.

6. Spankings must result in a changed, contrite heart. If there is no sorrow or change of attitude, we have only angered and embittered our child. Spankings must be strong enough, and applied wisely enough, to change the attitude.

7. Bring matters to complete resolution. The youngster should have a total understanding of what he or she did wrong and make a complete apology. We should then extend our full forgiveness. If this does not happen, we risk the creation of a sullen, brooding rebel. The air should be clear and our relationship completely restored when everything is over.

8. Do not spank for every offense. Spanking is not always called for, nor does it work as effectively on all children. Some kids are virtually oblivious to spankings, and others are totally crushed by them. Use another form of discipline if it works better. As children enter the elementary school years, spanking becomes increasingly less appropriate.

9. Start as soon as a child begins to understand the word "No." At approximately fourteen months or so, our little ones begin to understand us. As soon as they do, they begin to assert their wills against ours. At first, we simply need to speak firmly to our children and then physically move them or the object that is the problem. There will come a time, though, when a light slap on the wrist or thigh along with a strong "no" is needed.

In closing our thoughts on discipline, let me make three very important suggestions.

First, *be consistent.* Establish some basic rules and limits and stick to them. Do not allow moods or weariness to affect your standards. It is extremely frustrating to our children if we consistently change our position. Put up the "fence" and leave it there. To vacillate on issues of discipline will embitter and discourage your kids. You will lose respect, and they will become increasingly sullen and defiant.

Second, *parents must always be unified on disciplinary matters.* Never argue with each other in front of the kids about discipline. If the kids see that you are divided, it will create havoc beyond belief. They will play you against each other, and it can threaten the very life of your marriage. Work out mutually agreed standards in private, then back each other up. Talk things out. Come to unity. If need be, get responsible advice to help resolve disciplinary differences. Also, when you see that your spouse is frazzled, weary and irritable, step in and give him or her some help in dealing with the kids. It's a team effort and we need each other.

Many of you reading this book now realize that you are going to have to crack down and that there are going to have to be major changes. The problem for some of you is that your kids are older now and are not accustomed at all to the strong discipline they need. This brings us to the third thing we need to do: *Make a definite plan.* My suggestion is to have a family meeting, and using the appropriate scriptures, talk about God's plan for raising kids.

Be sure to present and teach this in a positive manner. Don't use the Bible only to warn or correct; help the kids to see the loving plan of God for them and for your whole family. Go over a few of the changes that will need to be made, have a prayer, then get started. Don't tackle everything at once. Select your battles carefully. If you get too picky or try to change everything overnight, you will drive yourself and your kids crazy. Start with some basics, and build up from there.

When it comes to discipline, many parents fall into one of two extremes. They either practice something much more akin to child abuse, or they go to the opposite end and neglect discipline altogether. I suggest that you reread this section several times and study carefully the scriptures that have been referenced. It is vital for your children that you properly understand your responsibility and wisely and lovingly provide the correction and discipline they so much need.

Geri and I often said in the midst of raising our kids that we were working on four PhD degrees—one for each of our children. And, to this day, we haven't got a diploma hanging on our wall. Nothing else you ever do will cause you more anxious nights, more questioning of yourself, more wondering if you did the right thing than raising your children.

Read your Bible, pray your heart out, learn from the examples of other families, get good advice from people who know what they are doing, and you will see progress. God is our Father, and he is still working on helping *us* to grow up. He knows what a hard job this is, and he will help us get better and better at it.

God's Training Plan

Train a child in the way he should go,
and when he is old he will not turn from it.

Proverbs 22:6

Principles

Training is different from discipline. By nature, it is proactive, whereas discipline is reactive. With training we *build*, with discipline we *alter*. Both are absolutely essential. Attempting to raise kids by discipline alone, without training, creates negativity and frustration. On the other hand, training without discipline is foolhardy and weak and underestimates the rebelliousness of human nature. As parents we must become equally proficient in both areas.

To get a better view of the concept of training, let us examine in depth the passage which best articulates this wonderful concept:

> Hear, O Israel: The LORD our God, the LORD is one. Love the
> LORD your God with all your heart and with all your soul
> and with all your strength. These commandments that I give
> you today are to be upon your hearts. Impress them on your

129

> children. Talk about them when you sit at home and when
> you walk along the road, when you lie down and when you
> get up. Tie them as symbols on your hands and bind them
> on your foreheads. Write them on the doorframes of your
> houses and on your gates. (Deuteronomy 6:4–9)

Let's break it down and discuss the key phrases:

'These commandments' (v6)

The Bible is the undergirding basis of all training. It is the
very word of God, to be revered, loved and believed by us all. It
is the standard which has authority over our children and us. It
is a wonderful thing to be taught the Bible from infancy. Some
of us act as if this is somehow a disadvantage. Far from it. Think
of the millions of young people that have been horribly scarred
forever because they were reared godlessly with no moral standard.

Both we and our children should consider it a priceless privilege, not a detriment, to be raised in a home where the Bible is
taught. Such was the home of young Jesus, and of young
Timothy, of whom Paul said "from infancy you have known the
holy Scriptures" (2 Timothy 3:15).

'Love the Lord your God' (v5)

Training flows from a relationship of love with a personal
God (see chapter 1). Training emphasizes a life that pleases God,
not simply conformity to a standard. If we teach our kids the
Bible with a "do-it-or-else" mentality, we have missed the point.
The Bible should not be opened up only when we want some
extra authority to straighten out a child; instead, it should be
used continually to teach kids about who God is and about his
great plan for their lives.

'These commandments...are to be upon your hearts' (v6)

Training at the heart level is the only way to bring our children to God and to effect lasting change. Look to mold your children's hearts, not just their actions. To be able to do this, our own heart must be devoted to God. Only as we keep our inner selves pure can we deeply impart God's word to our children. The Word should be written "in their hearts and...on their minds" (Hebrews 10:16). Share your heart with your child. Love God, love his word, help your kids to take it deeply into their hearts, and then they will never let it go.

'Impress them on your children' (v7)

Training with the Scriptures must be done with great conviction, sincerity and earnestness. If you casually read off some passages and talk about a few ideas, you will get nowhere. Kids know what is important to you. If you want your training to stick, you will have to give it all you've got.

'Talk about them when you sit at home...walk along the road...lie down...get up' (v7)

Train constantly—anywhere, anytime, any place. It is meant to be a natural part of life. Training is not the dreaded "lecture" kids sit through and forget about as soon as it is over. It is not nagging our kids about their misdeeds. Training is the wonderful experience of teaching our children about life while we live it—that's what makes it fun, effective and doable. Some of us think of training as if it were classroom instruction or a counseling appointment. If we confine it to this, we will never get the job done. The fact is, we just can't raise kids by appointment. Most of the teaching Geri and I did was spontaneous and occurred during the normal activities of life.

Such training makes spiritual things real and down to earth to children. If we lapse into a vocal "holy tone" when we decide to be "spiritual" and teach the kids about God, they will blow us off as religious phonies. If the only training they are getting is in a scheduled discipling time or at church classes, it will not be nearly enough.

We must never underestimate how many times we will have to say the same things over and over. Develop your own catchy sayings that you repeat continually in your family. Don't be discouraged. They are learning, even if at times it seems they are not. It is the nature of kids (and all of us) that the same things have to be taught repeatedly. As I have often said, "Life consists of learning the lessons you should have already learned."

Specifics

What are some things we train into our kids?

Character

All of us have a basic temperament. Start very early with your kids, building upon their good points and strengthening any areas of weakness. They should begin to learn who they are, the good and the bad, pretty soon in life. Teach them early on to "cleanse the inside of the cup" and not just put on an act.

> Even a child is known by his actions,
>   by whether his conduct is pure and righteous.
> (Proverbs 20:11)

Beliefs and faith in God

Even though your children are raised in a Christian home, they will have to come to their own faith and their own convictions about what they believe. If your kids start wondering if they really believe in God, in Jesus, in the Bible, and in the teachings they have heard in church, don't panic or think you have failed. This is a natural and needed part of maturing. If you overreact, you will short-circuit the process and drive your kids underground. Welcome it as a part of their learning to love God not just in heart and in action, but with their mind as well. Your role is to share your own faith and convictions with them while they are little, and to help them grapple with their questions as they grow up.

Attitudes

Train a faithful, positive, "can do," winning spirit into your children. Teach them to love life, to expect the best, to be glad that God made them just who they are. Teach them to expect God to work powerfully and that there is never a reason to remain discouraged.

Values

Good morals, such as honesty, sexual purity and the avoidance of drugs should be taught and explained. Teach these values while the children are very young, and they will never forget them, and likely never abandon them.

Personality, demeanor and manners

Train your children to have pleasant personality traits. If a child has a grating or offensive manner, don't let it go unaddressed. Some of us need to realize that our kids really aren't that likable. Their personalities are offensive. If you spot this, deal with it; if others point it out to you, check it out; then take action.

Don't let your kid grow up a social outcast because of a rude, abrasive or weird personality. Some kids think they are hilarious when they are not; others are pushy or act strange to get attention; some are withdrawn, bland wall flowers. Help them with these kinds of things, all the while being careful not to break their confidence.

Teach your offspring to have a pleasant countenance, to look directly at people in conversation and to have a positive, happy spirit. Don't let them be a negative, complaining sourpuss!

Train in things such as politeness, table manners, hygiene and social graces. Crass, rude or wild youngsters who smart off, tease, bully, destroy other kids' possessions and create mayhem while visiting in other people's homes must be confronted, disciplined and helped by their parents.

Work ethic and responsibility

Hard work and a sense of responsibility are habits of character that can be trained into a child. Laziness is a serious flaw that forever will mire them in the morass of underachievement. Therefore, teach and inculcate an ethic of hard work.

Geri and I used the book of Proverbs liberally on this great subject:

> A sluggard does not plow in season;
>   so at harvest time he looks but finds nothing.
> (Proverbs 20:4)

> The sluggard says, "There is a lion in the road,
>   a fierce lion roaming the streets." (Proverbs 26:13)

> As a door turns on its hinges,
>   so a sluggard turns on his bed. (Proverbs 26:14)

We stressed repeatedly with our children that they should learn to "love hard work," and that nothing worthwhile was accomplished without diligent effort.

School work is a character issue. If you train your kids to work hard, be responsible and do their best, school will, in all likelihood, never be a serious problem. Are they giving it their all? Are they working hard? If they are, the grades will usually take care of themselves. We never made grades a huge issue in and of themselves—that is the wrong focus. Instead, make diligence and excellence the issue.

Challenge your kids to be disciplined, to pay attention in class, and to do their very best work. Then you can be proud of them, based on their effort. Usually, unless there is some other problem, their grades will be fine—probably well above average, since so many kids in their classes aren't trying very hard.

Give appropriate jobs and responsibilities around the house. Early on, get the kids to make their beds, clean their rooms, and put up their things. Household chores such as setting the table, sweeping, folding clothes and doing dishes should be assigned fairly. A word of caution: don't let your harder working kids do everything for the others. And don't you do everything for them either!

Our kids all had jobs to do, and they learned to tackle them with gusto. They came to enjoy the after-dinner clean-up as a fun time. Make it a goal of your training that doing jobs and serving in the home is not a battle, but a habit. To help with this, we gave the kids allowances apportioned to their age, the responsibilities they had and their faithfulness in carrying them out. This brings us to the next key element in training.

The Reward Concept

Remember, training is a proactive, positive concept. It lessens the need for continual discipline and correction by filling up a child's life with good. Use the concept of reward to build in positive traits. For younger ones, make charts so they can earn stars for good behavior and be rewarded by a prize after accumulating a certain amount. We found that the more motivated, stronger-willed and difficult the child, the greater the need for tangible goals and rewards.

Geri discovered this with Elizabeth when she was very young. They were fighting so many battles over attitudes that Geri created a chart with the desired actions written down on the left and with a grid to the right. Every desired behavior was followed by the word "happily." It went like this: "Gets dressed *happily*;" "Goes to bed *happily*;" "Brushes teeth *happily*," etc. At the end of the grid was a picture of a long-desired, incredibly amazing lunch box that would be awarded to Elizabeth after she accumulated fifty stars (Geri wisely allowed her to select the reward for herself).

Elizabeth's attitude and behavior changed radically. It was a joy for us and for her. After much hard work, she proudly went to school with her brand new lunch box—and we promptly fixed up a new chart!

The concept continues to work as children get older. As Elizabeth matured, we found that she still did her very best when she had a goal for which to shoot. Parents, praise good behavior and reward it with increased freedom and privileges. Reward may just be the final tool you need to make your training a success: "Do not be overcome by evil, but overcome evil with good" (Romans 12:21).

Training is an irreplaceable part of God's plan in raising children. We cannot overstate its importance. Parents, we don't have to spend our lives on the defensive, always correcting our children's mistakes and disciplining them. Nor do we have to fume with frustration or wring our hands in worry.

Instead, we can take the initiative. We can put all that energy into training. Training is the key to becoming a positive, faithful parent who makes a difference—a lifetime difference—in the life of a child.

> Buy the truth and do not sell it;
>   Get wisdom, discipline, and understanding.
> The father of a righteous man has great joy;
>   He who has a wise son delights in him.
> May your father and mother be glad;
>   May she who gave you birth rejoice.
> (Proverbs 23:23–25)

Chapter 8

Nurturing Confidence in Children

For you have been my hope, O Sovereign LORD,
my confidence since my youth.

Psalm 71:5

Take a trip back into your childhood and remember some remark or incident that especially damaged your confidence. Do you recall the sense of self-disgust, shame and embarrassment that swept over you? Chances are, even as you remember it now, those very same emotions will cause your pulse to quicken and your face to blush. As parents we often forget the pain and difficulties we endured in our formative years as we sought to build some sort of identity and security.

One of my most embarrassing moments happened when I was in the eighth grade. (May God protect middle-schoolers!) The county fair was in town, and I got up all my courage and asked the girl down the street out on my very first date. To my amazement, even though she was taller than I, she said "Yes"! I was excited beyond belief.

After much agonizing, I decided on my outfit: blue jeans, white shirt, white socks, penny loafers and a sporty new corduroy red vest. (Let the reader understand: to wear the Red Vest was a declaration that one thought oneself worthy of the designation "cool." Since I was new to this school, I was hereby laying it all on the line.)

When the big day finally arrived, I was so nervous that my breath came in short, shallow gulps. My mother took us over to the fairgrounds and dropped us off. At first, everything went along nicely. We walked around, took in the sights, and tried to win some prizes—all the while ingesting generous amounts of popcorn and cotton candy.

Then we hit the rides. Now to say that I was susceptible to motion sickness is to vastly understate the case. As a matter of fact, I had been known to get queasy on Interstate exit ramps. I considered this fact for a moment, but felt somehow that my manhood was on the line, and so we sallied forth. It was to be the greatest mistake of my young life.

The Scrambler...made it! The Octopus (a much greater test)...made it...sort of. I began to feel a little woozy. I should have known better than to challenge my system again, but folly drove me onward to inevitable disaster. It happened at the very apex of the normally harmless Double Ferris Wheel. The wheel stopped, the seat rocked back and forth, the world began spinning, and yes...I lost it. Regurgitated. Blew chunks. Tossed cookies. Called Ralph. Hurled. Spewed. Barfed. My seat belt prevented me from leaning over the side of the car. My whole outfit, including the once glorious Red Vest, was now an obscenity. The tattooed guy operating the ride looked up and took it all in with a fiendish, leering grin. He left us up there rocking as long as he could before bringing us down.

I was an absolutely disgusting, revolting mess. I had to stay in that condition for what seemed an eternity before my mother came to pick us up. My date was actually very kind and compassionate, but I was humiliated beyond description. What did she really think? What would happen to me at school when this got out?

I tell this story to remind us how tough it was "back then." From that first trip on the school bus right down to the last hurrah at the senior prom, early life is one long struggle for self-esteem. Kids can be viciously cruel to one another. They will label and ridicule any aberration; they will call names, exclude, bully and tease.

If we are not watchful, we will be completely oblivious to the tremendous difficulties our children may be facing. Some of us need to wake up!

We cannot protect our kids entirely from the hard knocks of life, nor should we. What we can do, however, is give them the guidance and inner confidence that will enable them to overcome. As our children's primary mentors, we must help them develop both an unconceited confidence and a healthy humility. These are treacherous waters, and we will need wisdom and help from the Scriptures to navigate our way through them.

Wrong Foundations of Confidence

Let us first identify the false foundations, so that we might not build on a faulty foundation.

Physical appearance

From day one, we are judged and judge others by appearance. According to the standards of a particular society, people are attractive, so-so or homely. Tall or short, fair or dark skin, straight hair or curly, petite or large...you fit in or you don't. Many kids spend huge amounts of mental energy trying to figure out if they look good, or bemoaning their supposed ugliness. For some children, coming to terms with their physical appearance is one of the great battles of life.

My wife has seen my old pictures from elementary school, and she says I was a cute kid. That is certainly not the way I felt about myself. I was too short and had big ears, red hair and freckles. I was sure that everybody else (with the possible exception of my mother) thought I looked really dumb. Only later in life, when I read my Bible and came to admire young David, who was short and had red hair, did I begin to think that maybe my appearance was okay.

Many parents have been taken in by the world's standards of judgment. We overvalue beauty. We make it a big deal. When we do so, we are setting up our children for problems. They will gauge their own self-worth by their appearance and will judge others that way as well. What happens when someone better-looking comes along? What if they should ever suffer a disfiguring injury, and what happens as they age, and their body is not what it used to be?

To build confidence on a solid foundation, you first need to give God the credit for every gift your child has, including any gifts of appearance. Believe it yourself, and teach it to them continually. This gives a child assurance but also gives them a sense of humble appreciation.

Second, teach them to value the inside above the outside as God does:

> But the LORD said to Samuel, "Do not consider his appearance or his height, for I have rejected him. The LORD does not look at the things man looks at. Man looks at the outward appearance, but the LORD looks at the heart."
> (1 Samuel 16:7)

Athletic prowess

Very quickly, kids notice who is faster, stronger and more coordinated. Such children are generally more popular and usually become leaders, especially among boys. Being athletic is a wonderful gift, but is not a valid basis for the judgment of character.

Consider some of the great athletes of our time whose personal lives are totally lacking in virtue. No, being gifted with speed, strength, endurance and agility is not the ultimate good in life. We have said in other places in this volume how important it is for children to develop physically, but they must not judge the worth of themselves or others on that basis.

Intelligence

"Aren't you smart!" we say about our bright little one, and very soon in school the evaluation of brain power is a daily occurrence. Being called "dumb" or "stupid" ranks a kid right at the bottom of the social ladder. The fact is all of us have known some awfully foolish smart people, and their high I.Q. only made them worse! *Wisdom* is the quality God admires, and it is a product of character, experience and obedience to God—qualities that are attainable for all.

In raising our kids, Geri and I valued good grades, but we appreciated great effort even more. If our children were giving their best, then we encouraged and applauded them, no matter what the final outcome. We were aware of grades, and we rewarded them, but we believed it was a mistake to put the primary focus there.

Material possessions

The kid who has the coolest bike, hottest car, newest electronic marvel, latest video game or the most up-to-date clothes has a leg up in our society. It is actually quite amazing how many "friends" possessions can attract. The TV ads preach the message: "You've got to have this to be cool"—and we literally buy into that way of thinking.

We let our backgrounds bias us. Some of us grew up rich, others poor. We are horrified that our kids aren't dressed in the most expensive clothes—like we were as children. Or, we are determined that they will have the very best of things that we never had. How superficial and worldly this is, and how far from God's way. Jesus said:

> "Watch out! Be on your guard against all kinds of greed; a man's life does not consist in the abundance of his possessions." (Luke 12:15)

Don't let your kids grow up thinking they are better or worse than others because of what they have or don't have. And remember: it is fine to be generous with your kids and let them dress fashionably, but they must not have their confidence in or their focus upon mere outward appearance.

Mistakes Parents Make

In addition to building on a wrong foundation, there are other errors we can make that undermine our children's confidence. Listed below are nine of the most common:

Being basically critical

If you mostly see the negative things about your kids, then that is what they will see about themselves. If you think the best way to motivate them is by telling them they are no good and harping on their mistakes, you are dead wrong. This may be the way you were treated by your parents, but please do not repeat this sin with your kids.

Others saw Simon son of John only for what he outwardly seemed to be—an emotional, unstable hothead; Jesus saw him for what he could become—a great leader and a man of faith. Jesus even changed his name to Peter, the "Rock." And that is just what he became.

Failing to teach and train

Go back and re-read the previous chapter. Start taking the time to teach and to train your kids, and the results will amaze you. Your children will grow in confidence as their skills and personalities improve. You will reap the side benefit of becoming much closer to your children, and you will earn their gratitude as well.

Failing to express specific esteem, praise and admiration

A generalized expression of love is just not enough. We must say what we love, like, respect and appreciate about our kids in very understandable, concrete terms. "Son, you did a great job cleaning your room. You are a hard worker." "Honey, you are so encouraging to others. You have a great smile." The more specific is our praise—and the more often—the better.

Spending little or no exclusive time

Kids form their self-esteem based upon the kind and amount of time we give them. If we are always "too busy," they will conclude that they are unimportant and worthless. For those of us who have larger families, this will take some real planning and effort. Some kids are difficult, demanding and emotional and require lots of attention. But we may have another child who is laid back and doesn't seem to need us as much. Don't be deceived—all kids needs time alone with their parents.

Failing to understand unique needs

Children, like adults, are motivated or discouraged in different ways. We must become students of our children's personalities to discover how best to build them up. In my family, for

144

example, Alexandra responds more to affection and encouragement, whereas Elizabeth is inspired by challenging goals. David wants time to hang out, then he feels encouraged; Jonathan likes to be encouraged, then we can go hang out. (And yes, they are all from the same gene pool!)

Showing favoritism and comparing

Let's say you have two sons—one is an athlete, the other a musician. Do you applaud the achievements of one more than the other? Some of us do, simply because of our personal preference. Or you have two daughters—one is a straight-A genius, and the other is an average student but is a leader and is very active in service clubs. If you try to challenge either one by comparison to the other, you will breed frustration, jealousy and bitterness. Instead, appreciate and commend the strengths of both.

Pushing too hard, too soon

If you are a highly motivated achiever, be careful that you do not burn your kids out before they hit the third grade. They are just children, you know! In my four years coaching soccer, I saw some parents ranting and raving on the sidelines, pushing their kids as if their ten-year-olds were playing for the World Cup. In my first team meeting with the parents, my speech went this way:

> "Look, these are just kids. They are here to play a game. Here are our team priorities: (1) have fun, (2) make friends, (3) learn how to be team players and be good sports, and (4) learn to play soccer. Believe me; we will do our best to win our games. But please, *let them be kids!*"

I think I was one of the most fired-up coaches in the league, but it was the fire of enthusiasm and zeal, not of winning at any cost. With this emphasis, our teams won two championships and were in the playoffs the other two years, but mostly, we had fun doing it. Whatever your kids' talents, let them enjoy what they do, and let them enjoy their childhood while they are doing it.

One more practical observation: be careful before pushing your kids ahead of their age group in school. Some kids might handle this well, but others may not be emotionally or socially mature enough to function well around older kids. In some cases, if their age is close to the cut-off date, it may even be better to hold them back a year before they enter first grade. We did this with our two boys and never regretted it.

Parental self-degradation

Humility is one thing—lack of confidence in who we are before God is another. If you verbally downgrade yourself in front of your children, you hurt their view of life and of themselves. They will imitate you in viewing their faults as being greater than their strengths.

Living our lives through our children

Let God guide your offspring into the path he chooses for them. Don't try to live out your own dreams through your children. And don't try to make up for all you failed to accomplish by pushing your kids into things they don't really care about. I wish I had played more organized sports as a youngster, but I refused to pressure my boys into it on my account. I tried to encourage and inspire them in athletics, but I never wanted them to have the feeling that "Dad will be disappointed if I don't do awesome in sports." Give guidance and direction, but please, let's keep our own pride out of the picture!

The Right Foundation

The only proper foundation for a child's confidence is his or her relationship to God. If they look to God and his unconditional love, they will develop a confidence that is not cocky and a humility that is not self-hatred.

> And so we know and rely on the love God has for us ...Love is made complete among us so that we will have confidence on the day of judgment...There is no fear in love. But perfect love drives out fear. (1 John 4:16–18)

How to Nurture Confidence

Here is a list of nine practical helps to building godly self-esteem:

Stress relationship to God

Teach them that they are special in God's sight and that he is with them in all they do. He made them just the way he wanted, and he has a great plan for their life.

Focus on character above looks, talent, intelligence and possessions

Over and over again, tell your children that it is heart and attitude that matter most to God. I have a saying: "Character always wins out in the end." Talented kids may dazzle their way to the top, but without character, they will come crashing back down.

147

Applaud effort more than ability or achievement

In the parable of the talents (Matthew 25) three men were each given different amounts of money, each according to his differing ability. The two successful men were equally commended by the master even though one produced more than the other. Let it be so in your home.

Encourage openness about their fears, insecurities and failures

Kids are often burdened with anxieties, insecurities or a sense of failure. They may hide it from you and even from themselves. Watch, listen, notice. Ask them if they have anything on their minds that they need to talk about. When they open up to you, work them through things until they are confident. I have found that sharing some of my blunders and failures as a youngster helps my kids to see that everyone makes mistakes. Their faces light up, and they say "Dad, did that really happen? What did you do about it?" This draws me closer to my kids and assures them that they are not alone.

Encourage achievement and provide opportunities to grow in their areas of natural strength

Search out your kids' strengths, and develop them. Everyone has been gifted by God in some area, yet so many people go through life thinking they have no talent (cf. Ephesians 4:7, Romans 12:3-8, 1 Corinthians 12:12-26).

Others make Herculean efforts to succeed, but in a field that is removed from their sphere of ability. No matter how hard they try, they come up average simply because they are out-of-pocket. Your job is to help your children discover and succeed in those things for which they are best suited.

Help them improve in areas of weakness

Encourage your children to be well-rounded. Don't let them totally withdraw because they feel inadequate or awkward. For example, your children may not be the best students—their talent may lie in athletics or in people skills. Don't let them give up on their grades and just become a "jock" or a popularity freak. Academics are too important to neglect simply because they don't come easily. The same thing is true of other areas as well.

When I think of the great men and women of the Bible, I see people who had excellent talents but broadened themselves so that they could make a better contribution. Consider the woman of Proverbs 31, whose skills ranged from homemaking to business and management; consider David who was a shepherd, soldier, military commander, political leader, songwriter, musician and singer. Encourage your children to have their special expertise but to be interested and knowledgeable in many things.

Help them form encouraging friendships

The circle of friends around your child can build or break confidence. All young people need to belong to a group that affirms and accepts them. It is devastating for a child never to fit in or to always feel inferior and on the "outs." Some kids try to hook up with groups or individuals that basically do not accept them and constantly put them down. If you see this happening, you need either to teach your children how to act differently, so as to not turn people off, or you need to steer them towards a different group.

Don't be afraid to monitor your children's friendships. We always told our kids, "If you can't help someone be better, or if either one of you makes the other a worse person, then you cannot be close friends." We said it, and we enforced it. We have an obligation, especially with younger ones, to protect our children from the tease, the bully, the kid who ridicules or the child who is a bad influence.

David once had a friend like this in our neighborhood. The kid was not intimidating or threatening, he was just critical of David all the time. He was a year older, and therefore was stronger, faster and more coordinated. He would point this out and take digs at David for not being able to match his awesome feats. It was done quietly and subtly, but I finally noticed what was going on. I pulled David aside and asked him how he felt about it. He assured me that all the talk didn't bother him, but I still urged him never to let it hurt his confidence.

Geri and I started monitoring the relationship more, and we diminished the amount of time the two boys spent together. We encouraged David to play with kids his own age and provided more opportunities for that to occur.

Through the years, all of our children had friendships with wholesome kids from excellent families in the church. We made the effort to overcome any obstacles of distance or inconvenience to make this happen, and it paid off. Even when someone moved, we encouraged the keeping up of these friendships by phone, writing and special visits. We also sent our kids to the regional church camp. Many of the friends they made there are still in their lives today. These relationships with other "Kingdom Kids" are incredible in their influence for good in our children's spirituality, happiness and confidence.

Teach them to appreciate and applaud the efforts and achievements of others

Children who learn to admire and encourage others will be confident. They are strong enough to give credit when credit is due. They see that others are not their rivals but are their friends and companions. Friendly competition is good, but always having to win is bad. Nobody likes a sore loser who whines, sulks and gets angry when defeated; nor do people like a cocky winner who rubs it in when victorious.

Teach your kids to give their best and never to blame the teacher, their teammates, referees and/or selection committees when they lose. If they can "rejoice with those who rejoice," they will learn to accept themselves, accept life, and still be confident.

Teach your kids the example of young men like Jonathan, who could have easily been jealous of David, but who instead became his best friend and greatest encourager (1 Samuel 18). Teach them about John the Baptist who said that Jesus had to become greater, and he had to become less (John 3:30).

Be basically encouraging

Be your children's biggest fan. Tell them you think they are awesome—and they will be! Praise the pictures they bring home; look at and encourage them in their homework; applaud their efforts in all their endeavors. Let them feel the tremendous warmth and backing that only a parent can give. If you are fundamentally positive, then even when you do give correction, it will be more likely received with thankfulness rather than discouragement.

Someone has said that it takes five compliments to overcome one criticism. I don't know the exact numbers, but I do know that human nature flourishes with a diet of praise and that it shrivels when fed with continual blame. If your kids feel they have your blessing and approval, their confidence will soar.

$

In Psalm 23 David speaks of the faith he had as a boy. "The LORD is my shepherd, I shall not be in want" (Psalm 23:1). What confidence, what assurance, what peace resided in this young man's heart. It is no wonder, then, that when the great moment of challenge came, as Goliath stood defiantly before the cowed army of God, that this courageous, innocent teenage hero rose up. He based his confidence upon the victories of his boyhood:

> "The LORD who delivered me from the paw of the lion and the paw of the bear will deliver me from the hand of this Philistine." (1 Samuel 17:37)

The connection is obvious. The simple faith he developed in the days of his youth was the quality which catapulted him to greater things. He prepared himself and his moment came.

Build that kind of faith and godly confidence into your sons and daughters, stand back and watch what God will do!

Part 3
Fabric

Chapter 9

Foundations of a Spiritual Family

> But as for you, continue in what you have learned and have become convinced of, because you know those from whom you learned it, and how from infancy you have known the holy Scriptures, which are able to make you wise for salvation through faith in Christ Jesus.
>
> 2 Timothy 3:14–15

What do we mean when we talk about "a spiritual family"? Perhaps we should begin by discussing what we mean by the term "spiritual," and go from there.

Paul uses this word to describe a level of maturity that is beyond the early, immature stages of discipleship when we still think, react and behave more as we did before we became disciples of Jesus (1 Corinthians 3:1–4). He also says that those "who are spiritual" are capable of restoring Christians who have fallen into sin and are able to "carry each other's burdens" (Galatians 6:1–2).

Although Jesus does not use the term "spiritual," the teaching he gave in the Sermon on the Mount is a perfect definition of what it means to have this great quality. Simply put, it means to be on the inside what we are trying to do on the outside: to be genuine, not to live a pretense of religious performance but to function out of a sincere relationship with God.

A spiritual family, then, is a family where God is honored and where his presence is sought and experienced in daily life. It is a home where prayer is an ongoing reality and where the Bible is faithfully read and obeyed. It is a family who honors God with a total commitment of life and heart—a family that is dedicated to following Christ. It is a home that loves God's church and is fully involved in its fellowship and ministry. It is a family who has times of worship, praise and study. It is a place where the children, as they mature, are coming to love and learn the Bible and where the parents are working with each child to disciple them to Christ. And finally, it is a group that seeks to help others become disciples of Jesus.

This is much more than a "good" family, a "nice" family or even a church-going family. A family can be all of those things and still not be spiritual. To be spiritual is far more real and infinitely more powerful. A spiritual family is the "salt of the earth," "the light of the world," "a city set on a hill," whose example is such that other people notice and give glory to God. To be a spiritual family is a wonderful and powerful thing.

A spiritual family must be led by spiritual parents. We cannot take our families where we ourselves have not gone. As was pointed out in chapter 1, children can spot a fake a mile away. Therefore, we must be genuine in our love for God, consistent in our walk with him, and wholehearted in our dedication to his cause if we are to have a godly impact upon our kids.

What are the things we must incorporate into family life if we are to be spiritual? We will discuss six basic areas: prayer, discipling times, family devotionals, devotion to the church, an evangelistic lifestyle and children's quiet times.

1. Prayer

As parents, we should lift up our children before the throne of God always, praying that he might protect them, guide them, save them, and one day take them to heaven. We should imitate Paul, who said of his prayers for Timothy, his son in the faith, "Night and day I constantly remember you in my prayers" (2 Timothy 1:3). We must realize that we have a powerful and relentless adversary who wants to destroy us and our family as well. He will stop at nothing to take our children away from God. Our prayers are perhaps the most powerful weapon available in their spiritual defense.

I am reminded of Jesus' words to Peter on the night of his betrayal and arrest, when knowing that Peter would confront the full power of Satan, he warned him:

> "Simon, Simon, Satan has asked to sift you as wheat. But I have prayed for you, Simon, that your faith may not fail. And when you have turned back, strengthen your brothers." (Luke 22:31–32)

"But I have prayed for you." These words of Jesus show the difference prayer can make in the battle for the souls of our loved ones. Parents, we need to be prayer warriors on behalf of our children. We are in a battle for their souls, and our prayers can turn the tide.

But we must pray *with* our children as well. They will learn to pray by hearing us pray. They will learn to experience God's presence as they see it is real to us. We should pray with our children at regular times such as bedtime and mealtime—not in a rote or routine manner but from the heart. Geri and I often prayed with our kids as they stepped out the front door on the way to school. In our home in Miami, this developed into a neighborhood event. The other young boys on our street began to notice what we were doing and gathered around our front door every morning to join in our family prayers as they headed off to school.

We also have family prayer just before we get out of the car to go into church services. It helps everyone get into the right frame of mind. Since Geri and I often have speaking assignments, we ask the kids to pray for us. I'll never forget one of the prayers of my son Jonathan: "God, help my dad to do an awesome sermon, and please dear God, help him to *think* he did an awesome sermon!" (My son knows all too well that I am my own worst critic!)

In times of difficulty or great challenge, the family should be in prayer together. The children learn that we are totally dependent on God to help us and that we can do nothing without his blessing. One way we accomplished this in our family was by setting up "prayer partners." When there was something of particular concern on our heart, we would team up with one of the kids and get them to pray about it, and we would reciprocate by praying for some special need of theirs as well. The answers God gave built our faith and bonded us closer to our kids.

What if you have a young child who does not want to pray at bedtime? We faced this from time to time with our kids, and my wife developed some strategies that always seemed to work. First, she would talk to the kids about how God was a real "person" who loved them and wanted to be close to them, and that even though they could not see God, he was always nearby. If the resistance to praying kept up, her next step involved their beloved bedtime song. Geri would say, "Well, if you don't want to pray, then you're probably just too tired for your bedtime song as well. Good night. I'll see you in the morning!" This wise tactic usually resolved the problem instantly.

2. Heart-to-Heart Spiritual Conversation

We return now to a concept introduced in chapter 7. We need to learn how to talk about spiritual things with our children, and to do so regularly, freely and openly. Reread Deuteronomy 6:4-9. In our judgment this is the single most important teaching in the Bible on how to impart spiritual truths to children and how to build a spiritual family.

The key is open, continuous and heartfelt communication. This is the spiritual conversation that threads its way through all of our interactions with each of our kids. It is the weaving of biblical teaching into the very fabric of our family life and our children's hearts. It is the kind of teaching Jesus did with his disciples, who were "with him" (Mark 3:14) almost constantly for three years. He taught them day in and day out as they went about living real life. This is the great thing about being in a family—we are together in the living of life for years. God intends that we take this opportunity to impart spiritual truth to the minds and hearts of our kids. Mostly, we do this as we go about our normal activities.

I don't know about you, but for Geri and me this realization came as a relief. If we had had to schedule in times to teach our kids, we would have gone crazy. We did schedule some specific times, and they were helpful, but most of our teaching was done during our normal routine: meal times, riding in the car, doing odd jobs around the house, hanging out, relaxing, playing and talking.

When we impart spiritual truths in this way, kids function better and learn more readily. They see that walking with God is real, and is for real people, and not reserved for the super-religious. Knowing God is not something to be compartmentalized into a segment of our life: it *is* our life.

It is about knowing, trusting and loving some*one*, not just doing some*thing*. It is not defined by going to an activity, or being some weird, otherworldly religious person. It is being in a relationship with a personal, loving Heavenly Father who also happens to be the creator of the universe.

In all the years of teaching and volumes of writing we have done on parenting, I don't know of anything that Geri and I have tried to communicate that is more important or less understood than this. It is the key to everything. In summary: speak to your children about your faith and love for God, and speak to them from your heart to their heart. And do this as you go about everyday life.

That having been said, there is a place for scheduling regular times to discuss spiritual matters with your kids. If you are a working parent, and as your kids get more and more involved in their own activities, you may find that sheer practicality demands that you set time in your schedules for each other. Geri did not have to do this because she was at home more than I and was proficient at easily moving in and out of spiritual conversation. She also was adept at using times like the early morning, the arrival home from school and bedtime to get into great talks with the kids.

Since I was often away from the house during those times, I found that setting an individual consistent time helped me to better connect with the kids. I never had to do this with our firstborn, Elizabeth, because I could devote myself to being with her when I came home from work every day. I would oftentimes gather her up and go for a walk or play with her in the back yard, and we would have good talks during those precious moments.

But as the number of kids increased, I learned that setting a weekly time to collect one the kids and go out for a drive, a walk or a visit to a local coffee shop was invaluable. Even then, I tried to make these times as natural as possible.

For example, I took our youngest child, Alexandra, to school on Friday mornings, and we would stop at a coffee shop along the way. She would have a bagel; I would have a cup of coffee, and we would talk. I never had to plan what to talk about—although Geri would sometimes clue me in on what Alexandra was dealing with that week. I would come up with a verse we would read and discuss together, and we would pray while driving to school.

Those times are some of my best memories of my relationship with Alexandra as she grew through her teen years. It was simple, it was easy to do, but it made all the difference in the world.

Simply put, these "discipling times" are times you spend alone with your children to talk with them, teach them the Bible, and pray with them. When your children are young, it will obviously be on a very limited scale—just a short Bible verse and a prayer is all he or she needs.

As they get older, you can gradually lengthen the time, although it should never go too long for their limited attention span. Never let these times become a boring, burdensome duty. They should be enjoyable, relaxed times of learning and close-ness for both of you. You may want to go someplace out of the house, even if just for a walk in the neighborhood, a visit to the park, or to go out and get a soft drink.

Select topics and verses to help the children with their cur-rent needs. Geri and I often compared notes to help each other determine what the needs were. Read the verses together, talk about them, and make some application. You can even commit some part of the Scripture to memory. At dinner whoever was learning a new verse would sometimes share it with the rest of the family.

Let God lead these talks in the direction he wants. You may have selected a topic but then realize that the kids need to talk about something else. Don't over-think what you need to do, and don't over-plan. Let it flow; let the Spirit lead. Use the opportunity to pray together.

So, in summary: you will have a spiritual family by weaving God and spiritual things into the fabric of your daily life. And, if you sense you need to do so, you can schedule regular times with kids to be alone and have good talks. The value of these open, heart-to-heart conversations with our children cannot be overstated. It is not that complicated, and we can all learn how to carry out God's simple, but effective plan. We will cover how to have heart-to-heart conversations in chapter 12. But let's get started now, and let's learn how to speak to our children from the heart, and to the heart!

3. Family Devotionals

> From there he went on toward the hills east of Bethel and pitched his tent, with Bethel on the west and Ai on the east. There he built an altar to the LORD and called on the name of the LORD. Then Abram set out and continued toward the Negev. (Genesis 12:8–9)

Family worship is a powerful and necessary feature of a spiritual household. Family devotionals are those times when the entire family gathers to sing, pray, study the Bible, draw near to one another and worship God. It is a chance to have our own worship service—to be a small church. There is no feeling quite like gathering in our own home with those we love to draw near to God together. When we do, we know that the Lord himself is with us, as he promised:

> "Again, I tell you that if two of you on earth agree about anything you ask for, it will be done for you by my Father in heaven. For where two or three come together in my name, there am I with them." (Matthew 18:19–20)

What a wonderful promise, and what a beautiful experience for a family to have! We would have guests in for our devotionals from time to time, and they would often tell us how encouraged they were by being there. It is God's desire for all families to experience the joy of worshiping him together. Family worship can turn the entire atmosphere of a home for the better.

Family devotionals should be anything but a boring, irrelevant ordeal to be endured by dutiful parents and restless children. They can and should be dynamic, fun, down-to-earth and creative. Some of you are already starting to feel inadequate—but stay with me; this is not that hard to do.

We suggest that you plan the devotional with your spouse, being careful to select a subject relevant to the current needs of the family. Don't just go through the motions, but use the time to address any important behavior or attitude issue. This is not to say that we should always employ the time to correct everyone. If you allow your family devotional to turn into a weekly lecture, you have gotten off track. While it can be a time to address problems, use it primarily as an opportunity to worship, teach and inspire. Utilize it to paint a picture of the way things in your family can be and will be by the power of God.

The younger the kids, the shorter the devotional. Our sessions lasted anywhere from fifteen to forty-five minutes. Geri and I usually planned them, but sometimes we sat back and allowed the kids to take that role. We had a pattern we generally followed, but were careful not to get into a rut. We usually began with a few minutes of singing. We varied the selections from the high-energy kids' songs to the most beautiful hymns of worship. Sometimes we took out the songbooks and taught the kids some new songs. I would often have a short Bible lesson, seeking to draw out plenty of discussion. We often did role-playing and acted out Bible stories. We usually closed out with prayer, and tried to give everyone a chance to join in.

Our topics for devotionals covered every conceivable subject. We studied the parables and the different incidents in Jesus' life. On one occasion we discussed Jesus' teaching on being a servant-leader in Matthew 20:20–28 and declared the following week to be "servant's week." We acted out many of the great Old Testament stories, such as Aaron and Hur holding up Moses' arms to win victory in battle (Exodus 17:8–13). We acted out the four kinds of disobedience (defiant, disarming, deaf and dreary) that we shared with you in chapter 6 of this book.

Some nights we would share about answered prayers. Other

163

times, if someone was having an especially discouraging week, we would put them in the center and have a special prayer for them. There are many outstanding resources you can use if you need some ideas. Above all, don't feel intimidated or burdened—keep it simple, enjoy these times, and God will bless your family accordingly.[1]

4. Devotion to God's Family, the Church

Our family's relationship to our local church is a crucial building block in growing a spiritual family. The Bible teaches us to "love the brotherhood of believers" (1 Peter 2:17). The church is God's family and is the place in which we serve him on a day-to-day basis.

Really, the church is an extension of our own family, a part of the larger family God has graciously given us. It follows then, that we should love God's church and that as parents we should cultivate that same sentiment in our families.

Parents, how we look at church is crucial to how your kids look at it. If you have positive, loving attitudes about the church, your kids will too. In our family, the kids knew that we loved God's people and that we loved to be at church activities. Church, to us, was "we" and not "they."

As a result, our kids did not develop bad attitudes about attending church services. On the contrary, they loved going to church. Their best friends were there. They loved the worship services, and they enjoyed their Bible classes. If we ever noticed that things were not being done excellently in the kids' ministry, we pitched in and helped to make it better. I would urge you to do the same. Don't sit back and say, "Why don't 'they' do this better?" It is your church; help make it better yourself.

---

1. We recommend using Tom and Lori Ziegler's *As for Me and My House: 50 Easy-to-Use Devotionals for Families* and *As for Me and My House: 50 Easy-to-Use Devotionals for Preteens and Young Teens*, both published by DPI.

Teach your kids to respect their Bible class teachers and to honor and appreciate their youth or teen workers. These people should be their heroes. Don't withdraw from church or church activities because of the misunderstandings that occur and hurt feelings that come up between kids from time to time.

Don't become part of a gossiping clique. Don't let your kids become outsiders, malcontents or troublemakers in the youth group.

If they have a conflict with a leader or with another kid at church, make sure they solve it quickly. If you ever have a problem with someone or something at church, solve it in a godly way. Don't speak inappropriately in front of your kids about it. If you do, you will undermine their love for God's kingdom, and you will reap a bitter harvest from what you have sown.

5. An Evangelistic Lifestyle

When something is a blessing to us, we naturally talk about it and share it with others. Sharing the good news of Jesus should be a part of our everyday family life. The more our kids feel blessed to be in our home, the more they will want to help other families learn about God.

Some of us separate our families from our outreach to others. Let's remember that our families are some of the brightest lights that God can use to illuminate a dark world. It blows people away when they observe a happy, loving family with respectful, obedient kids. It is so rare that they will want to know why our family is the way it is.

Have people into your home. Draw people into your family life. Let them meet your children. You won't even have to say anything; they will see a difference. And when they do, you can tell them where it comes from. It is great to see God use your family to change the lives of others.

6. Children's Walk with God

Early in life, we need to help our children cultivate their own relationship with God. He must become real to them, a friend and companion who loves them, is always with them, and who constantly watches over them. For children raised in Christian homes, we have a great opportunity to help them do this from infancy. It is a great opportunity, but there are dangers and pitfalls that go with the territory. It is possible that they go through the motions of going to church services and attending all the functions but not come to have a personal heart for God. Christianity can seem to them to be a burden to be borne rather than a relationship to be enjoyed.

To overcome this, they must come to know and love the one who is issuing the call to commitment. Having their own time of prayer and Bible reading is one of the best ways for them to learn to know God and enjoy him personally. Time spent alone with the Bible and in prayer provides children the opportunity to develop their own faith.

This can sound onerous and dutiful (to us and to them), but there are ways to help our kids learn to enjoy and look forward to spending time with God. Start them out with very small steps. As they mature, it can be helpful to suggest that they read a few verses from Proverbs or a short psalm and have a brief prayer as they prepare to go to school. Make it simple, helpful and practical.

Geri and I taught our kids to use the quiet moments alone with God to come to know him for who he is. We encouraged them to go outside, to look around at the beauties of nature, and realize that God made it all—that he is powerful, wise, and yet very concerned for them as individuals. This has helped our kids to look at God as someone who can be loved as a friend and not just as a master who wants their obedience.

In the younger years of preschool and early elementary school, you may want to sit down a couple of mornings a week and have brief quiet times with your children. As they get older, in later elementary school age, they can begin to have these times on their own. We recommend that kids start out spending just a few minutes per session, divided between prayer and Bible study. Later, you can teach them to keep a private journal where they write down the things they learn.

If Jesus' own disciples asked him to teach them to pray (Luke 11:1), then our kids will need some help as well. It might be helpful to teach your kids to pray with some sort of pattern. We have found the ACTS pattern to work well for kids: Adoration, Confession, Thanksgiving and Supplication. (Be careful: those are some pretty big words!) Be sure to go through each topic, explain exactly what it means, and how to pray in that area.

As your children get older, direct them to study books like Proverbs, Psalms and the Gospels. Have them study the lives of the youth and teens of the Bible such as Joseph, Samuel, David, Daniel, Miriam and Mary. Keep up with how it is going to make sure they are continuing to learn and aren't getting bored. If that happens, give them some ideas to help them make things exciting again.

There are many variables in all of this that cannot be addressed in this book. You will have to study the personality and character of your children to determine their levels of maturity and spiritual readiness. You can make a mistake either way: by pushing them ahead too quickly, you can overwhelm your kids; by not challenging them enough, you leave a vacuum in their hearts that can be filled up by the world. Pray for wisdom, get wise counsel from spiritual people, and trust God to guide you.

$

These are the building blocks to use in constructing a spiritual household. No one does it perfectly, and all of us will feel

167

inadequate at times. Get started, and be patient—it takes years to do this job. And, no matter how well you do it, there is always something else to work on.

Take it one day at a time, lay one brick at a time, and in the end, we will have a house that stands firm and strong, and one in which we, our children, and God himself are happy to dwell.

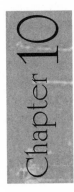

Chapter 10

A Close Family

His brothers...hated him and could not speak a kind word
to him.

Genesis 37:4

How good and pleasant it is
when brothers live together in unity!

Psalm 133:1

I once asked a policeman friend of mine what situation faced
in the line of duty frightened him the most. I expected to hear
something about drug busts or armed robbery, but instead, the
reply I received was "domestic conflict." At first I was surprised,
but after thinking about it for a while, it made sense.

Is there any place on earth where our passions run deeper
and our weaknesses are exposed more than in our own homes?
It is here, with those closest to us, that our nerves become raw
and our hearts become embittered. It is in the home, where we
have given our deepest love, that the hurts penetrate the most
painfully.

I would encourage you to sit back sometime and listen to
what is being said under your own roof. Turn on a recorder,
place it in a corner, and forget it is on. Play it back later and note
carefully what you hear. Listen to the words and to the tones of

voice. Most of us would be amazed and embarrassed to know how we, and our children, address one another.

Let's face it—many families are not that close. Tension, bickering and quarreling rule. There are explosive arguments and simmering feuds that go unresolved indefinitely. And even if there is not much outward conflict, a family can merely coexist without deep love or enjoyment of one another. If fighting and bitterness is the downfall of one family, shallowness and superficiality is the cancer that slowly consumes the soul of another.

Even when we search the Scriptures for answers, we find more of the same. Consider the story of Cain and Abel, the first murder in history, committed by a man's own brother. Look at Jacob and his twin brother, Esau, set at odds by the folly of their parents' favoritism and driven from one another by their greed, envy and desire for revenge.

See how the sin continues into the next generation as Jacob's sons turn against their younger brother, Joseph. They conspire to send him away as a slave and cover over their plot with the fabrication of his accidental death, leaving their father heartbroken in grief for years. Look at the family of David, torn apart by lust, rape and incest, with one brother murdering another and then leading a rebellion to take away his father's throne.

Do we need to see any more to convince us of the horror of a divided house? It is as if God is saying, "I will give you an answer to your problem, but I first want you to see how terrible and awful are the consequences of a disunited and warring family." It ought to cause us to humble ourselves, get the help we need, and make the changes we must make.

Thank God there is a better way. The choices parents make can turn the tide. For some of us, it will mean a radical change in what we accept and in what we expect. But with prayer, proper training of the kids and patient determination, it will happen.

There are four keys to having a close family, and we will discuss each one in turn. The keys are respect, openness, fabric and atmosphere.

1. Respect

We discussed the importance of children's respect for parents in chapter 5, but here we refer to respect that must exist among everyone in the entire household. How can we have it?

Eliminate critical, harsh talk

I am shocked by the kind of talk that some parents allow in their families. Our conversation sounds more like a TV sitcom than that of a godly Christian household. We accept this kind of talk as normal, even though we know what the Bible says about it. Perhaps it has gone on so long that we are desensitized to its brutality. Perhaps we have come to believe that speaking in a kind and respectful manner is an unattainable ideal, and we do not even make the effort to change. But change we can, and change we must, if we are to have a close family. Consider the following scriptures that have to do with communication:

> Reckless words pierce like a sword,
>   but the tongue of the wise brings healing.
> (Proverbs 12:18)

> A man who lacks judgment derides his neighbor,
>   but a man of understanding holds his tongue.
> (Proverbs 11:12)

> A gentle answer turns away wrath,
>   but a harsh word stirs up anger. (Proverbs 15:11)

> Do not let any unwholesome talk come out of your mouths,
> but only what is helpful for building others up according to
> their needs, that it may benefit those who listen. Do not
> grieve the Holy Spirit of God, with whom you were sealed
> for the day of redemption. Get rid of all bitterness, rage
> and anger, brawling and slander, along with every form of
> malice. Be kind and compassionate to one another, forgiv-
> ing each other, just as in Christ God forgave you.
> (Ephesians 4:29–32)

Paul says there are some things we just plain need to "get rid of." No fanfare, no playing around—just get rid of them. We must get rid of *harsh words*. Name-calling and words like "stupid," "dumb" and "shut up" must go. Some of us are using and permitting far worse language than this, language that I cannot put in print. May these words of Jesus warn and sober us:

> "But I tell you that men will have to give account on the day
> of judgment for every careless word they have spoken. For
> by your words you will be acquitted, and by your words
> you will be condemned." (Matthew 12:36–37)

We wouldn't think of speaking to people outside our family circle in that way. We might not even talk that way if we had guests in our home. And, let me ask you, would you use the same words if Jesus were in the room? Let that be the test.

We must get rid of *harsh tones of voice*. We need to remember the words of Paul, who told us that love "is not rude" (1 Corinthians 13:5). A sneering tone, dripping with scorn, contempt and sarcasm is just as wrong as cursing. Many of us speak this way as a matter of habit, and we allow it to go on among the kids as well. Some kids can utter a supposedly harmless statement with enough venom to kill. This must be stopped, and it can be stopped.

We must get rid of *harsh actions, looks and expressions.*
Communication is far more than words and voice—it is done
with the entire body. Slamming doors, throwing things, stomping feet—all of these actions say what we really feel. The Bible
talks about "haughty eyes," and it says that God detests them
(Proverbs 6:16-17). When the kids roll their eyes at us or at one
another, it is a sign of contempt and disrespect. It must be rec-
ognized, confronted and eliminated from their behavior.

Cultivate respect and appreciation

This is the second major step in building respect into your
family life. In the previous section we addressed the need to
remove the bad, now we speak of how to replace it with good.

Family devotional times provide a great opportunity to teach
our children lessons on mutual respect. Geri and I employed
every Bible story and verse we could find to illustrate this all-
important habit of thought and behavior. Respect and appreciation will not just happen by accident; every family has their own
battle to fight. It comes down to a matter of what we expect of
our children and persevering in our training of them. Sometimes
in our home it felt as if we were fighting a losing battle, but we
worked long and hard, and it paid dividends of peace and joy
that were beyond price.

Another way to cultivate respect in the home is to encourage
its expression in words. Again, this is where family devotionals
can help. We often had entire sessions focused upon "building
up one another." We would go around the circle and give each
of us an opportunity to build up other family members. We
would tell of the ways we had seen each other (Mom and Dad
included) change and grow. We had "thank you nights" when
we shared our gratitude for specific things family members had
said or done.

Sometimes we began these sessions in anything but a happy

and an appreciative mood, but as we began to encourage each other, it wasn't long until our spirits lifted, and the bad feelings were replaced by hugs and tears of joy. God designed us to flourish when we are respected and appreciated. Encourage your family to begin doing so, and watch the atmosphere change to one of joy and brightness.

> Pleasant words are a honeycomb,
>   sweet to the soul and healing to the bones.
> (Proverbs 16:24)

One last brief piece of advice before we leave the topic of respect: teach your older children how to lead their younger siblings, and the younger ones how to follow them. The larger the family, the more valuable this will be.

2. Openness

> Instead, speaking the truth in love, we will in all things grow up into him who is the Head, that is, Christ. (Ephesians 4:15)

For a family to be close, open communication is a must. Many of us do not realize the frustration and desperation that exists in our children's hearts because they do not feel free to talk with us. Establish an open door policy. Help the kids feel confident to bring up anything on their minds, at any time they feel the need.

When they want to talk, give them your full attention. Take the time to listen, learn and consider before you give advice. If it is something unpleasant, take care not to jump to conclusions, get angry or overreact before they have a chance to tell the whole story.

What do kids need to talk about? Younger children have a myriad of things going through their little heads that we need to help them with. They may have hurt feelings—and parents may be the ones who did the hurting. They might have an ongoing difficulty with a sibling or a playmate. They could have a problem with their school work or with a teacher, or a bully may be picking on them. There could be something on their consciences, even from many days past that they need to confess. Their needs range from the trivial to the gravely serious—and we need to hear them all.

What about older children? In case you don't already know, as children get older, it only gets more intense! The earlier you establish the habit of open communication, the better. The issues older kids deal with include dating, sex, drugs, conflicts with friends, weird thoughts, grades, appearance and issues involving their spiritual life. It can be exhausting, but it is a wonderful thing to sit down and talk heart to heart with your children, and to experience the closeness that results. (See chapter 12 for more on having heart-to-heart talks with our kids.)

But the need for openness is not limited to parents with the children—it also includes the children with one another. A simmering backlog of unresolved problems, issues and conflicts undermines family unity. In working with adults, I am amazed at how many siblings remain estranged from one another since the days of their childhood. Make a commitment to not let this happen between your children.

Geri and I made it our practice to never allow conflicts between our kids to go unresolved. When we became aware of a problem, we found that sending the kids off by themselves to talk it out worked beautifully. Sometimes we had to mediate, but more often than not, completely on their own, the kids emerged from these talks smiling, happy and reconciled.

There will certainly be times when our kids don't want to talk to us. And, some kids will struggle more than others with stuffing their feelings. But if we allow a child to habitually brood, carry resentments, and hold in their true thoughts, we are sitting on a time bomb. It will go off sooner or later, and everyone in the family will be hurt.

Consider for a moment the stories of two of the most tragic figures of the Bible, King Saul and Judas Iscariot. Saul was a brooding, tormented man who was filled with jealousy and envy. Instead of working through his temptations honestly, he held in his feelings. A reading of 1 Samuel 18 reveals that his pattern was to think one thing, but to say another. (Does that describe any of your children?) His turmoil increased, resulting in his complete emotional and spiritual breakdown.

With Judas, we have a similar story. Read through the Gospels, and look for the words of Judas. There are virtually none. Contrast that with Peter, who was completely outspoken and whose outbursts got him in trouble on just about every page. Both men had their weaknesses, but which one overcame them? The one who was open!

As parents we should be just as concerned about the child who holds everything in as the one who blurts it all out. The latter can be helped, but the former lives in isolation and his or her problems may go unsolved.

Have open talks during your family devotional times. Keep the air clear. Establish an atmosphere of freedom and openness. You will not lose authority by hearing what is on everyone's minds; you will instead create a happy, relaxed and righteous family.

3. Fabric

By fabric I refer to building a structure and a rhythm into our family schedules. For families to be close, they must have regular times when the whole group gets together. During those hours we build an identity and a feeling of our own little society that is just "us." It is this feeling of group togetherness that makes a family a family, and that makes being in it one of the most joyous experiences on earth.

I am afraid that some of us might not even know what we are shooting for. We may not have experienced it in our homes growing up, and we do not have a clear picture in our minds. But don't be discouraged. If we try, we can learn. When and how can we create a fabric for our families that will hold them tightly together? Let me suggest several ways to go about it.

Use mealtimes

We all have to eat somewhere, sometime. Why not do it together? It is a natural time to stop what we are doing, gather around the table, sit down, enjoy a meal, and have a great time being with one another.

Our family loved mealtimes. Because of the different schedules of the kids' schools, having breakfast and lunch together was usually not possible for us. So, we made it our habit to have dinner together. To this day, our kids remember with fondness our family dinners.

Here are some suggestions:

Try to have everyone in the family there. Take care not to let the family meal be eroded by the encroachment of outside forces. Sit down to eat at the same time. Turn off the TV and cell phones, and take off all head sets. Now, the family may converse!

Dinner conversation is actually a learned art. Sometimes, things may get a little disjointed, and you are not as "together" as you could be. On one such occasion in our family, when Jonathan was around two, he was feeling left out, and to get back in the middle of things, he turned to me and asked, "So, Daddy, what did you do today?" We all got the point, and it led to a standard practice. We established the habit of telling the significant things that happened to us during the day. The kids started enjoying this so much that they would save up special news to share with the entire family at dinner time.

This seems simple, doesn't it? Maybe too simple. But the simple things are what build fabric into a family, and they are the stuff of which memories are made. Set a dinner time and honor it. This means that our family practice is to sit down at the table and eat together, rather than leaving the food on the stove for everyone to serve themselves whenever they have a chance. Cease letting people read the paper, watch TV, or do their homework during dinner. Disallow the grabbing of plates and running off to eat in separate rooms. No more setting up appointments that take you away from your family during the evening meal. Allow no phone calls during this hour. Make dinnertime an event, work hard to keep it special, and watch your family draw closer.[1]

Create family traditions

There ought to be some things that our family does that are uniquely "ours" and that bond us together in a special way. These activities don't have to be expensive or elaborate, nor do they have to take up large amounts of time. You don't need to plan out what your family traditions are going to be—they just kind of invent themselves.

Our family loved it when I made pancakes on Saturday mornings. I couldn't always do this because there was usually quite a bit of activity scheduled on Saturdays. But whenever I

---

1. Some families may have to be more creative and flexible than others in finding times to spend together. Jobs and other responsibilities may make adherence to the dinner hour difficult or even impossible. But what must not be sacrificed is regular time together, time that the whole family is committed to and counts on. What we must avoid is allowing societal or self-imposed pressures to weaken or destroy our family life. If extra-curricular school activities or job responsibilities are harming or making our family life a shambles, we need to honestly re-evaluate their worth, and make any changes necessary in order to build a close family.

did, and everyone was there, it was a blast. As each of the children came along, they got to help me fix the meal. I treasure the memories of each one sitting on the kitchen counter in their pajamas, helping me hold the electric beaters, and splattering batter all over the place. I really didn't put anything special into the recipe, but I got rave reviews. Geri loved it—all she had to do was sit down, talk and enjoy the food. And I even did the dishes.

Holidays and birthdays

Look through your Old Testament sometime and check out all of the feast days and celebrations that God planned for his people. Do we get the point? We need holidays, those special times of being together that our families can look forward to all year long.

We made birthdays a big deal for each family member. The kids didn't always get a big party (four per year was too much for the checking account), but we always made birthdays a special time for everyone. After we had the cake and opened the presents, we went around the family circle, telling what we loved about the birthday person. This made birthdays more than just getting presents, it made them times of tears, laughter and love that just could not be replaced. If we could not have afforded to buy a single gift, we could have had this tradition, and afterwards felt we had all been blessed and encouraged.

I don't know what holidays your family holds dear, but our family loves Christmas—and always has. The kids had a scripted set of Christmas moves that we had to follow, starting with going out to buy the tree. We all had to agree on it—a major decision, to be sure—and afterwards they had to run around and play hide and seek in the Christmas tree lot.

After we brought the tree home, we had a chili dinner. Then the boys and I set up the tree and put on the lights, and Mom and the all of the kids did the decorating. After the tree was all done, we turned out the lights in the house, plugged in the lights on the tree, sat admiringly in front of our beautiful handiwork, and had an eggnog toast.

I'm actually getting a little tired remembering all the work. But the point is this: our families need times and traditions that define us. They make us who we are. They are the great markers of our year. They will be what we remember, and are what our kids will most likely one day pass on to their kids.

4. Atmosphere

By atmosphere I refer to the overall tone of a home—the feeling we have living there day in and day out. For a family to be close, the mood must be positive and pleasant. It is impossible for a family to be united, tight and together when the atmosphere is bad. What do we need to do, then, to create this kind of feeling in our home?

The basic attitude of being optimistic and joyful is essential to creating an encouraging atmosphere. We ought to have the conviction in our homes that "God is with us, life is great, and no matter what happens, we're going to come out ahead!" Life can be difficult at times. There are many setbacks and disappointments along the way for parents and kids. If we continue to trust God and stay faithful on a daily basis, even in the "little" things, the whole family feels better and feels closer to one another.

As the leaders of the family, parents set the tone. If we become negative, the family will not be as close. When we are gloomy and anxious, we cannot provide the spark and inspiration to pull the group together to accomplish great things.

Don't let a sour, negative child ruin the atmosphere of a home. There is nothing worse than for one whiny, complaining sourpuss to be allowed to spoil your good times. No one wants to be around someone like this. Kids won't enjoy dinner or family devotionals with their sibling frowning away from the sidelines. It may require a lot of energy and love from you to keep dealing with these kinds of attitudes, but you must not give up or accept a complaining spirit.

But we must be more than positive and joyful, we need to start having fun and laughter in our home if we are to have an atmosphere conducive to closeness. We need to kick back, relax, and have some great times, especially when there have been some difficulties and hardships.

Consider these verses:

> A happy heart makes the face cheerful,
>   but heartache crushes the spirit. (Proverbs 15:13)

> All the days of the oppressed are wretched,
>   but the cheerful heart has a continual feast.
> (Proverbs 15:15)

> A cheerful look brings joy to the heart,
>   and good news gives health to the bones.
> (Proverbs 15:30)

> A cheerful heart is good medicine,
>   but a crushed spirit dries up the bones. (Proverbs 17:22)

In our family, we did plenty of things to get the laughter going. Sometimes at dinner we had "Joke Night," when everybody got to tell their latest joke. Some were really lousy, but that was all part of the fun. The kids even begged to hear the old jokes they had heard me tell countless times before. They especially loved to hear stories of all the dumb things I have done and all the embarrassing things that have happened to me.

It is amazing how having fun brings a family closer. If we can laugh with each other, at each other, at ourselves, and at life, we will be close. Laughter and fun have a way of breaking down the barriers and letting us be ourselves, without pretension. It helps everyone to feel accepted, loved and at home.

But besides the atmosphere of attitude, the physical environment needs to be pleasant. When the home is bright, cheerful and inviting, it helps everyone feel good about being there. We need to keep our houses clean, neat and orderly. It's hard to feel great about being together when the place looks like a bomb just went off. Dirt, filth and clutter do not create an atmosphere of closeness. When the environment says "we don't care," then people stop caring about each other.

If God was concerned about the beauty and appearance of his home (the temple) then we, too, should be concerned about ours. My wife has always excelled at doing a lot with just a little money. By spending a few dollars here and there, and by carefully and skillfully arranging the colors, furniture, etc., she can transform a house into a place in which we love to live. We do not have to become materialistic or lose our focus on God to have an attractive home. It just takes some thought and extra effort.

In a world torn by division and loneliness, a close family is one of the greatest blessings we can ever enjoy. It takes a lifetime of effort, but no reward we receive in this world is any greater.

The psalmist David said it well:

> How good and pleasant it is
> when brothers live together in unity!
> ...For there the LORD bestows his blessing,
> even life forevermore. (Psalm 133:1, 3b)

Chapter 11

Anxious Parents

"So do not worry, saying, 'What shall we eat?' or 'What shall we drink?' or 'What shall we wear?' For the pagans run after all these things, and your heavenly Father knows that you need them. But seek first his kingdom and his righteousness, and all these things will be given to you as well. Therefore do not worry about tomorrow, for tomorrow will worry about itself. Each day has enough trouble of its own."

Matthew 6:31–34

Today's parents are anxious—I mean really, *really* anxious. I thought we Baby Boomers had set the bar for parental uptightness so outrageously high that no generation could possibly ever catch us. But, I am sorry to say, we have been left in the dust. The "parenting paranoia" of today's moms and dads makes us look like mellowed-out zombies by comparison. They have taken our worrisome ways to levels we never dreamed.

I suppose we shouldn't be surprised. Kids usually magnify their parents' weaknesses. In my book, any generation that awards kids a diploma in a cap-and-gown graduation ceremony when they complete preschool has some serious issues.

I hope you can forgive my tongue in cheek assessment of where we are today, and realize that I indeed do appreciate the devotion—amazing devotion—of this generation of parents.

But, parents, we are overdoing it. It is time to step back, take a deep breath, and take stock. This anxiety has its origins in two roots: conformity and competition.

Conformity

God's people are supposed to be different from the rest of the world. We are supposed to be *transformed*, not *conformed*:

> Do not conform any longer to the pattern of this world, but be transformed by the renewing of your mind. Then you will be able to test and approve what God's will is—his good, pleasing and perfect will. (Romans 12:2)

We are called by Jesus to be different from the world:

> "My prayer is not that you take them out of the world but that you protect them from the evil one. They are not of the world, even as I am not of it." (John 17:15–16)

We are, as Peter says, aliens and strangers here in this world (1 Peter 1:1, 2:11). And both James and John warn us not to love the world (1 John 2:14–16, James 4:4).

But, the temptation for God's people has always been to blend in and to let the world shape us rather than the other way around.

One of the ways the world most affects us is in how we raise our kids. We need to keep our spiritual priorities and principals properly ordered. Unless we are watchful, we can just mindlessly go along with what everybody else around us is doing, all the while giving no thought to spiritual principles and priorities.

When Jesus says that the pagans fretfully "run after" the wrong things, we can almost feel his eyes boring right into us worried, frenetic parents who ought to know better.

Competition

Competition with other parents and other families is one of the big producers of parental anxiety. Our guilt-buttons get pushed pretty hard if we feel our kids don't measure up. We think we are a "bad parent" if our offspring are not super-achievers perched at the very top of whatever ladder we think they need to climb.

So, we think we have to put them in every activity, every sport and every club under the sun. When we go this route, our parenting has become about us and not about our kids. We are functioning from a desire to prove ourselves rather than a passion to help our child reach their God-given potential.

Parents who push their kids hardest are often those who have regrets about their own perceived lack of accomplishment. Our own insecurities can so drive us that we use our kids to make us feel better about ourselves. Our kids are going to accomplish what we failed to accomplish; they are going to be who we never became.

Things change from generation to generation, sometimes for the better, sometimes for the worse. When I played pee wee football, my dad never came to a single game, and neither did many of the other boys' fathers. I have no idea why; that's just the way it was. Daddy took me hunting and fishing, but never showed up once for pee wee football. I never gave it a thought. It was just something we boys did together.

Nowadays, both parents feel like they have to go to every game—and they may have two or more kids playing in different leagues. If not, they feel as if they are being unsupportive. No matter that you are bone-weary or have other responsibilities to attend to, you'd better be on the sidelines at your kids' soccer games, or other parents will raise their eyebrows, and you will feel guilty. Can we stop and think about this for a moment?

Couldn't we explain to our little one at the season's get-go that sometimes Mommy or Daddy won't be at a game? Let's get a little creative—could we perhaps join with some other players' trustworthy parents and occasionally rotate going to some games, agreeing to transport and keep an eye on each other's kids?

Think about it. Wouldn't we in the long run be better people and better parents if we didn't try to live with such a jam-packed schedule? And won't it help teach our kids that the world does not revolve around them and their activities?

Jesus points out in the Sermon on the Mount that people in the world are consumed with worry. They worry about food and clothing; they worry about tomorrow. They just worry.

But spiritual people can worry, too. Especially do we worry about our kids. It may at first glance seem like parental responsibility, but it is often here that our continued attachments to the ways of this world reveal themselves.

Homework, Grades and Academics

Is it just me, or has homework gotten out of hand? Kids used to come home from school and be able to relax a little. Maybe go ride their bike, play in the back yard, grab a snack, have some fun. Now, if you go that route, you are in danger of academic catastrophe—and I'm talking about first graders!

Academics and learning are primarily an issue of character and discipline. It is a matter of simple responsibility to do the work they have been assigned to do, and do it to the best of their ability:

> Whatever you do, work at it with all your heart, as working for the Lord, not for men, since you know that you will receive an inheritance from the Lord as a reward. It is the Lord Christ you are serving. (Colossians 3:23–24)

If you will teach your kids to be responsible and consistent with their school work, grades will usually take care of themselves. Don't worry as much about the result as you do the effort and attitude behind it. If your kid is giving his or her best, applaud them. Such an effort will usually land them in an advanced place in the classroom. But if you become uptight about their grades, you will put pressure on your child and yourself, and the results will be bad.

When our kids came home with their report cards, we always took special note of the conduct grades. Those evaluations reflected directly upon the most important issue in their lives: their character. Those marks represented who my kid was, not just what they did. And if those marks were high, the academic grades came out fine just about every time.

If there is a problem with their performance, you need to address it. Perhaps your child needs to speak with their teacher and get some help. Maybe a certain subject is not an area of strength, or maybe they just aren't that motivated or interested. Whatever the case, there is always some way that you can help them take stock and improve.

Our son Jonathan had a hard time organizing himself and his homework. He would spend large amounts of time on unimportant points. He would end his study time having overdone one assignment to the neglect of another. He would get stuck and sit staring at the page as if glowering in frustration at a problem would solve it.

We figured that our job was not to do his work for him or with him, but to help him learn how to study and organize his time. Geri helped him set up a rough-and-ready schedule every afternoon—something like this: twenty minutes on math, twenty minutes reading his history book, thirty minutes working on the term paper that was due next week. To help Jonathan stay on track we got him a kitchen timer. He would set it at the time allotted for each section of his studies. When the timer went off, he had to move ahead. No matter that he had not quite finished; he had to go to the next assignment.

Then, at the end of every session he scheduled some time to clean up anything he did not finish in his original effort. He usually found that the time away from whatever he did not complete allowed him to come back to it with a fresh attitude and get past his earlier sticking-point.

I remember one father coming to me saying that in spite of his son putting in hours on his homework each night, he was still not getting it all done. His son just seemed unable to make himself move fast enough to finish his work each night. His grades were suffering, and the young man was getting more and more unhappy since he never had time to do anything but study.

I suggested to the father that he take a look at his son's homework and give him a reasonable time limit to finish it. After that time was up, he had to wrap it up. He could then play, hang out with the family, relax, or do chores, but no more studying.

I spoke to the dad a few months later. He was happy to report that having a set finishing time worked like a charm. The limits helped his son focus and get moving. He started getting more done, his grades went up, and he started having more fun as well.

Let us say it plainly: avoid doing homework *for* or *with* your children. When you function this way you are not helping them learn or grow in self-discipline. Instead of being personally involved, send them to their room or to a private, quiet place where they can work alone.

If you put them at the kitchen table so you can continually monitor their efforts, you are interfering with their learning how to discipline themselves. You are also going to wear yourself out. No, let them learn to work on their own.

If your kids aren't getting their work done, or are bringing home some low marks, figure out why and take appropriate action. But don't let that action be you hovering over them like a helicopter or sitting beside them like a watchdog. There are other things you can do to help.[1]

You can set up a reward system for a job well done. As our kids got a little older, we promised them a family dinner at our favorite steakhouse if their report cards came out good.

It might be effective to take away privileges if you sense there is a lack of effort.

There may be some other solutions. You can encourage them to speak to their teacher, or you can get them a tutor.

This is not to say that you can't personally step in on occasion to help with a problem, a project or a subject. But we cannot and must not intervene and start doing their work for them. Nor should we take upon ourselves the burden of being our child's conscience. So what if they get a bad grade? Parents, that's not the end of the world! Isn't that what grades are for— to let kids know where they stand and to motivate them to do better?

A few mediocre or bad grades can work wonders. Sooner or later, they will get the message: work hard, do your best, don't goof off. Hard work pays off with rewards—and not just good grades, but praise, encouragement and privileges.

I know what I am saying may seem like blasphemy. It certainly goes against the super-involved focus that many parents have, and the intense pressure they put on themselves and their kids. What I am trying to say is that by micromanaging and attempting to supply all the motivation, we take away our kids' need to motivate themselves. By hovering over them while they are working, we remove the need for them to discipline themselves. By letting them become consumed by homework, we take away the joy of learning and the joy of childhood.

---

1. We recommend *Ending the Homework Hassle* by John Rosemond (Riverside, NJ: Andrews McMeel Publishing, 1990) for an extended treatment of this subject.

Sports

Kids' sports programs have mushroomed into a vast network of leagues, seasons and competitions. In years past, most organized sports took place at school. There may have been some modest community leagues, but those games were usually played on a local field against other kids from nearby communities.

Most kids got into sports through informal games played in their own neighborhoods. There were no coaches and no manicured, lined fields; you had to squeeze the game into the vacant lot down the street. You made up your own rules. You selected captains who picked the teams, or you just numbered off and played with the team you got. There was no championship—you just stopped playing that sport and went on to whatever season came next.

And, there were lots of other games that didn't keep score: tag, dodge ball, hide and seek, red rover. You made up lots of games right on the spot—and those were probably the most fun. You had to work out your differences without a uniformed referee to blow the whistle and mediate. Lots of times on a disputed play, you just called a "do over."

The advantages of this kind of play should be obvious to us. Kids learn to use their imagination, and they learn to work together. They get to rest their minds and not be so controlled and adult-directed. They get to run free. Most of all, they get to be...kids.

Don't get me wrong, I am not saying organized sports don't have their place. Nor am I advocating turning back the clock. What I am saying is that over-organizing our kids and cramming their—and our—schedules full of sports can backfire on us. It can consume our time. And, most of all, it can rob our children of the carefree years of childhood and take away some their happiest memories and opportunities to grow.

Let's step back for a minute and look at the larger picture. What is the purpose of children's sports, anyway?

Here are a few:

Have fun

Have we forgotten the obvious? Sports are fun! They are not just about winning and keeping score. Sports are about the joy of play itself. They are about the exercise, the excitement, the craziness, the exertion, the burning off of energy, the laughter, the sheer exuberance of life. That is sport at its highest. Not everything has to matter. Kids need to play for the joy of play itself.

When we lived in Miami, I coached nine- to eleven-year-old boys' soccer. As I mentioned earlier in the book, I always gave a speech to the parents at the beginning of every season. In it I listed our team's priorities. The first on the list? *Have fun.* We found out that the boys were good at having fun, but the parents were not. You would have thought the TV cameras were rolling and gold medals were at stake, the way some of them behaved.

In our league we had some angry, cursing parents who berated their sons and the other teams—and my coaches and I would have none of it. We would not allow parents who acted that way to be near the sidelines. How many championships did we win? More than most. But mostly, we had fun, and that is what those boys remember to this day.

Make friends

Sports are a great way for youngsters to meet other kids and form the camaraderie that comes from playing together. The ongoing relationships with teammates last longer than the memories of who won and who lost.

Our three oldest children ran cross country in high school.

None of them was a star, but they loved hanging out with the other kids on the team. We still have friendships with some of the parents we met while our teens were on the team together.

Become a team player

One of the greatest values of sport is in learning the give and take of being on a team. There will usually be players on the squad who are better or worse than your kid. This is a great opportunity to teach our children to appreciate and respect the ability and talent of others. It is a chance to help them see that all talent, including athletic talent, is a gift from God, and that if someone else has more than they do, they can be happy for them and not jealous.

It is also a way to help our kids learn how to encourage those who may not be gifted in sports. We can help them to see that even though someone is the best and someone is the worst, every player on the team is valuable and has a part to play. If we can teach our kids to encourage and support the less capable teammate, they have learned a lesson that will make them a better person for the rest of their lives.

Learn how to win and to lose

Your kids will experience both in sports, and they need to learn how to do both graciously. To win and not gloat, and to lose and not sulk—how many adults could stand to learn those lessons?

Our oldest daughter, Elizabeth, was the first of our kids to go out for cross country. She has always been highly competitive, seeking to excel in everything she does. Although she was new to this sport, she set her sights on making the "top seven." (About forty girls from her school ran in each meet, but only those seven scores counted in the team competition.)

Elizabeth encouraged a quiet young lady from our neighborhood to come out for the team also. This girl was so talented that she became one of the top runners in the entire state. This was a step backwards from Elizabeth making into the top seven, but a real plus for her team. (And, her coach loved her for her recruiting!)

Elizabeth trained, worked, sacrificed, prayed and dreamed. But, she continually fell just short of her goal—she was always number eight. It was her senior year and her last chance to fulfill her ambition. Her opportunity came when one of the other girls in the top group was injured towards the end of the season. Elizabeth moved up into the top seven. Her dream had come true. And, to make it even sweeter, her team had a chance to place high—even to win—the season-ending regional competition. It seemed that her prayers had been answered, and things were finally going her way.

But, as the time drew near for the meet, her injured teammate recovered and began running again. Elizabeth's coach approached her and told her that even though the other runner had recovered, he felt that Elizabeth's dedication had earned her a spot on the team in the regional meet. Her place was secure.

Elizabeth started thinking. She realized that her team would have a stronger chance of winning if her teammate ran in her place. She struggled mightily with the decision, but went and told her coach that for the sake of her team, she would step aside.

Her coach, her teammates, and all the parents associated with the squad were amazed. Last I heard, her coach still tells the story to his team at the beginning of every season—the tale of the girl who trained hard and longed with all of her heart to run in the regional competition, but on her own gave up her place for the greater good of her school.

Elizabeth did more for her team, for herself, and for the cause of Christ by that decision than if she had run the best race of her life that day. It was a choice that helped to establish the way she would seek to live for the rest of her life.

Become more skilled in a sport that you enjoy

Sports are about learning. Enough said. It helps when kids get out there and learn something new. Some things come easy; others come hard. If our children learn to get better, to improve, and to get the most out of their talents, then they will take away something worthwhile from their participation. Sports are a great confidence-builder if we help our children to gauge themselves on how well they do with the ability they have to work with.

Keeping a Balance

There are so many sports leagues these days that it can be overwhelming to kids and to parents. If you have more than one child, it can be downright brutal. We had four kids, all of whom were involved in sports as they grew up. As our schedule began to be more and more crowded, we made a decision that served us well: *Each child could play only one sport at a time.* And, we also decided if you wanted to be in another demanding outside activity (such as the school play), then you were going to have to sit out that season in your sports league.

I'm just trying to be down-to-earth here. Parents, we all have to make some real-world decisions. Yes, you can decide! You don't have to just be swept along like every other family. Decide what kind of life you want to live and what kind of family you want to have. Kids' sports are your servant, not your master.

Our son David was pretty talented in soccer. He could have played at a fairly high level. But to do that he would have had to join one of the elite traveling teams, which meant more pressure on our schedule. We had three other children, all of whom had things they wanted to do as well. We desired to keep our family close, and above all we intended our household to be spiritually strong. We made a tough decision: *no travel league.*

David decided to run cross country instead. He did well and

194

made lots of great friends on the cross country team. He also had the time to participate in other activities like student government, the school play and the debate squad, all of which enriched and inspired him. We never regretted the decision, although Dad (Me!) being a competitive kind of guy, wondered from time to time what might have been had David stuck with soccer.

Some families can take on lots of stuff and still be tight-knit and spiritually strong. We knew we could not keep our most important priorities if we added any more pressure to our schedule, and so we made the decision we did. Our challenge as parents is to honestly assess what we can do and still keep Jesus as Lord in our family. Let that be your guide.

Another decision we made was that sporting events took second place to church activities. Our kids would not miss mid-week services to go to practice. We discussed this with our kids before they ever got involved, and we made this commitment early on in our family life. At the beginning of the season we or our kids let the coaches know what our family was all about and that while our children would be devoted and faithful to the team and to practices, church came first.

There were a few moments here and there, but it never became a problem. We sometimes made an exception if there was a championship event or the like, but those times were rare. Our kids won the respect of their coaches and their teammates, but most of all, they learned what was most important in life.

Summary: Priorities and the Pace of Life

All that we have been saying in this chapter revolves around what may be the most crucial issue in life: *priorities*. Most of us agree that God's purposes are more important than our own, that Jesus should take precedence over the world, and that building a close and loving family is a supreme value. For most of us, believing these things is not the issue—making it happen for our family in the real world is.

Listen to these verses where Jesus discusses the issue of priorities (emphasis mine):

> "Therefore I tell you, do not worry about your life, what you will eat or drink; or about your body, what you will wear. Is not life more important than food, and the body more important than clothes? Look at the birds of the air; they do not sow or reap or store away in barns, and yet your heavenly Father feeds them. Are you not much more valuable than they? *...But seek first his kingdom and his righteousness,* and all these things will be given to you as well. Therefore do not worry about tomorrow, for tomorrow will worry about itself. Each day has enough trouble of its own."
> (Matthew 6: 25–26, 33–34)

Jesus is not saying that concern for food and clothing is unimportant; he is saying that it is not *most important.* It is not that we seek nothing but God's kingdom; it is that we seek it *first.* And frankly, this is where many families go astray. It is not that we do not love God and his kingdom at all; it is that we do not love God and his kingdom *first.* Our emotions may tell us that surely God and his church are our highest values, but what does our calendar say? When crunch time comes, what do we choose?

If we begin to keep our kids home from services to study, what is really most important to us? And, furthermore, where is our faith? We can make the old argument, "We don't want to be legalistic," all we wish, but it is our observation that what seem to be small compromises lead to larger ones. We will wake up one day and find ourselves living a half-hearted Christian life, being nominal church members or "Sunday Christians," and then, too late, we will wonder why our kids have lost spiritual interest.

We can decide what kind of family we want to have. We don't have to live our lives like everyone else does. As a matter of fact, if we want to be Christians, we *must* not live like everyone else does.

Let's clearly set our priorities. Let's put academics and sports in their proper place. They are not the be-all and end-all of life. Jesus and his church are that. So what if our kids don't get into the elite school or star as winning athletes? In five, ten, twenty years, what will count? And, are not most of our anxieties due to misplaced priorities? Are not many of our worries engendered by having the wrong goals and skewed ambitions?

We live in perilous times. Money worries and a faltering world economy only add to the burdens parents have to bear. It is crucial to keep both our priorities and our faith firmly centered in Christ. We have seen, in the last few years, an increasing and alarming number of parents becoming more and more wrapped up in the world and its worries, and less concerned with building godly, Christ-centered families. It is the "little decisions" we make that determine whether or not our larger commitments are carried into our real lives.

And while there is no absolute guarantee any of us can lead our kids to Jesus, parents who have the greatest chance of seeing their kids come to faith are those who keep their priorities straight.

Most of us reading this book once made our confession: "Jesus is Lord." If we have faltered in our resolve, let us once again place Jesus in that sovereign place of Lordship in our personal lives, and in our families as well.

Much of what we have been worrying about will be cut down to size. When we put him first in our lives, we will find that Jesus is better, bigger and of greater worth than any problem we face.

Heart-to-Heart Talks

Give me your heart, my son,
And let your eyes delight in my ways.
Proverbs 26:26 (NASB)

Talking heart to heart is the secret of truly effective parenting. It transports us from the frustrating method of merely managing our kids' behavior to the powerful pathway of shaping their character; from the never-ending effort to dictate their actions to the greater work of molding their hearts. It enables us to know them as people—what they think, feel and believe in their deepest selves.

As a matter of fact, the better you know your children, the easier it is to raise them. It means you are working from the inside out. Practice this and you will realize one of the ultimate dreams of parenting: an intimate, close, satisfying, lifelong relationship with your children. Talking heart to heart makes all the difference in the world.

Maybe what we are about to discuss is an art. It is certainly more art than science. But, parents, it is an art we can learn. Yes, there can be a connection between the real You and the real Kid—soul to soul, heart to heart. Some of you may doubt you can attain this, but read on. You can learn, and so can they.

A Quiet Place

Raising kids and being in a family is a chaotic affair. Noise, interruptions, distractions—sometimes we can't even get a word in edgewise! And the more kids we add to the brood, the more intense it gets. Studies. Friends. Sports. Electronics. And, oh yeah, we parents have to go to work and even sleep sometimes. It may seem that talking on the heart level is utterly out of reach.

That's why, sometimes, we need to get away from it all. Even Jesus had to get away from his normal environment to spend time with his closest relationships:

> Then, because so many people were coming and going that they did not even have a chance to eat, he said to them, "Come with me by yourselves to a quiet place and get some rest." So they went away by themselves in a boat to a solitary place. (Mark 6:31–32)

If you want to speak intimately with your kids, take them away with you to a quiet place.

Get away to a coffee shop, go on a walk, take a ride in the car. In those kinds of settings our kids will find it easier to open up with us. This does not necessarily mean we have to be in utter seclusion. We may discover that an intimate, but not isolated, atmosphere is best. Sometimes the activity of walking or riding helps a kid to lower their defenses and tell you what is really on their minds. For boys, a campfire might just be the key to opening their heart. There is something about fire and men...

Being There

Sometimes it is not the kid who has a problem focusing; it is the parent. They want to talk, and we are distracted. We don't really make eye contact with them, or we go to the other extreme and have a glazed stare on our face. We are preoccupied by the newspaper, a book, the TV, household chores, our own thoughts...and the kids know that we aren't really there with them. We have to learn to be present, to be fully where we are at the moment, and nowhere else.

Most of us carry more anxiety than we know. It is all too easy to let the opportunity for a good talk pass us by because we are worried or preoccupied with our work even though we are home. I am a minister, and as such have a great deal on my mind all the time—or, at least I can have, if I am not careful.

Sometimes during dinner or at other family gatherings my wife will draw me aside and kindly whisper into my ear, "You aren't here." I am uncomfortable hearing those words, but ultimately I am thankful for being drawn out of my thought world and into my family's world.

It is easy to think that the concerns from work or about our finances, or even our own need to relax and chill out are more important than talking to our kids. They are immature, and their concerns seem trivial, and besides, they will be here tomorrow...so why not just put them off?

The problem is, if we continue to let those moments pass, our kids may finally give up, and over time we will drift apart. One day we will long to converse with them, but by then it may be too late.

Listen and Ask Before You Speak

My dear brothers, take note of this: Everyone should be quick to listen, slow to speak and slow to become angry, for man's anger does not bring about the righteous life that God desires. (James 1:19–20)

James's advice in the verse above may just be some of the most important we will ever receive as parents. Kids do and say things that cry out to be addressed. They disobey. They make mistakes. They forget. They irritate us. And, while it is certainly true that we as parents have much we need to say in raising them, there is also a time to listen.

It is easy for us to overwhelm and intimidate our kids, or just shut them down. We may feel that we have said just the right thing in just the right way, but we may have totally misfired, unless we know what is on our kid's mind. And the only way to be sure is to ask. Let's learn and practice the art of asking questions and of drawing them out.

Solomon has some good advice for us:

> The purposes of a man's heart are deep waters,
>   but a man of understanding draws them out.
> (Proverbs 20:5)

Try some of these kinds of questions and requests and see what happens:

"And then what happened?"
"And how did you feel about that?"
"What do you think about...?"
"Help me to understand about..."

Let's get all the facts before we render judgment. It may seem we have an air-tight case, but children need their day in court, and we don't always need to be the prosecuting attorney. Even if your kid is egregiously wrong, you will strengthen your ability to help if you take the time to get the whole picture before reacting. If our kids feel like we are always getting angry and flying off the handle, they may avoid us, start making excuses, tell lies, or just buckle on their armor and fight.

We have nothing to lose by listening for a while, maybe a long while. Even if our children are completely in the wrong, patiently listening will do far more to help us reach their heart than just blasting away. When they know their case has been fully heard, they are more likely to accept the verdict. And, by knowing their whole mind, we can address the real issues under the surface.

One of the hardest types of children to talk to is the one who just won't say much. Usually, this mysterious youngster is a member of the male gender. Somewhere along the way, even a talkative, outgoing young toddler can transform into a boy who is the mumbling master of the one-sentence reply or of the caveman grunt.

It will take every apparatus in your communication tool box to help this young man to open up. The direct approach may not work. It may be that he needs an extended time with us away from his normal environment before he opens up. Sometimes, he doesn't even know what he feels or thinks, or even what we mean by having a "deep talk." Whatever the case, don't give up trying to reach him. And don't despair—behind all that silence is a beating heart and a soul that needs to connect with yours.

If you watch and listen carefully, he may already be revealing more than you have thus far perceived. And, we must maintain the hope that some day, some how, if we are lovingly persistent, God will help him pour out his heart to us.

Try Setting a Regular Time

It might help us have more heart-to-heart talks if we schedule a regular time to spend alone with each of our kids. In our observation, this is an especially effective tool for fathers. Some kids, unless the occasion is pre-scheduled, will immediately start wondering if they are in trouble when we ask them to get together alone with us. Having a prearranged weekly or bi-weekly event takes the pressure off and also assures that we will indeed fit personal time with our children into our busy schedules.

The Four Family Pairings

Let's take a look at the different relationships in our families who need to talk heart to heart.

Mothers and daughters

Usually this pair has no problem talking. But, as girls get older, they may become more argumentative with their mom. Moms, you will have to let your girls grow up, have their own opinions and express them, even when they may be a little outlandish. Don't feel as if you have to respond to every immature statement. Pick your battles wisely, or you will be continually arguing with your daughter, and over some really silly issues. But when you need to address an important issue, do so, and expect to be listened to.

Mothers and sons

Mom, you may be the lifeline of heart-to-heart communication with your son. You may be his first resort, and his most trusted refuge. Boys who feel uncomfortable with and threatened by Dad may find it easier to bare their soul with Mom. If this is true, make yourself available to your son, and know that you have a unique and special place in his life.

But realize that it may take a while for a boy to open up, even with his mom. This is why you will need some time alone with him, perhaps while putting him to bed when he is little, or later, while riding alone with him in the car.

He may saunter into the kitchen while you are preparing dinner and just kind of hang around, hoping to talk. Treasure this special relationship, but also help him to open up with his dad. Don't let it be that your son only talks to you, especially about his problems with his father. You may have to guide him and teach him how to go about it. And, you may have to lend your husband a hand, as well. God has placed you beside your husband to help and complement him, and here is one place where you may be desperately needed.

Fathers and daughters

If fathers are even marginally warm, available and open, most daughters will take advantage of the opportunity to talk and be close. That's the good news.

Unfortunately, there can be a blockage, and guys, it usually comes from our end. Dads are notoriously distracted and "busy," or too quick to talk at, not with, their daughters.

Know this: if your daughter learns to talk to you, you can rest assured that she will thereby be saved from many of the pitfalls young women can experience. For instance, her open relationship with you will give her greater confidence in her relationships with boys—so much so that her vulnerability to sexual temptation is greatly reduced.

One of the roles a father can play in talking with his daughter is to provide a logical and reasoned pathway through her emotions. When my wife attempted to help my girls with highly emotional issues, I observed that feelings on both sides could get even more heightened. I discovered that I could in those difficult times provide a source of reason in a world that, at the moment, seemed out of control.

Fathers, this may be one of our most important missions in our daughter's life. Many is the time that a caring and loving father can help his daughter make sense of her own feelings, and find a way to understand and cope with a seemingly impossible situation.

Fathers and sons

This may be the most conversationally challenging of all relationships in the family. What we have here is a shared gender weakness. This is not to say that all men are failures at talking heart to heart, but let's face it—men usually struggle with this more than women do.

Untold numbers of men feel an immense vacuum in their lives due to the lack of closeness with their fathers. When you ask grown men what one thing they wish had been different in their relationship with their fathers, many will say, even with tears, that they wish they had had more heart-to-heart talks with their dads.

Fathers, let's learn from this, and not let it happen to our sons and us. Don't be fooled by appearances. If it seems your son does not to need to talk to you, he does. It may not even seem as if he wants to talk with you that much at all. Let's not repeat the mistakes that others have made. Let's take the time, make the effort, and learn the skills necessary to bridge that gap. Be encouraged—you can learn, and you can start learning now.

Not Always Intense

Heart-to-heart talks are not always negative or about resolving conflict. Far from it! They can be about sharing the things that are closest to our hearts with our kids. One way to help your kids open up to you is to appropriately share those things from your own growing-up years that could help them.

Let them know about some of your most embarrassing moments, your failures, your fears, your adventures, your relationship with your own parents—talks like these help your kids to see you as a human being and not just an authority figure. It also helps them to feel that they are not alone in their own struggles and insecurities.

What about sharing our emotions with our kids? This can be a complicated subject. But, being emotionally open usually doesn't hurt, and it can be a great help to let our children see our tears on occasion.

Sometimes we may need to keep our more intense feelings in check, especially when our children are young and incapable of understanding what we are going through. But as our children mature, it can help them be much closer to us if they see us tear up. Mothers are usually better at this than fathers, and it may be one reason why it is easier for kids to feel closer to Mom than to Dad.

If I may share my own experience...my children all tell me that they felt much closer to me as they grew up because I from time to time let them see my tears. I, like many men, was reticent to show emotion in front of my family, but doing so helped my children to feel closer to me, and freer to open their hearts to mine. My tears of loss helped them to feel compassion for me; my tears of sorrow for my mistakes helped them to forgive me; my tears of love as I expressed my affection for them, for their mother, and for God helped them to see how sincerely my heart was devoted to those who were most important in my life.

Perhaps the same will be true for you, and you will discover that allowing your tears to flow will open wider the door to your children's hearts as well.

Don't Be Afraid to Confront

When all is said and done, you are still a parent, and you are still in charge. We don't need to fear confronting bad behavior in a little one or reticent to take on a rebellious teen. We must not lose our confidence and become hesitant to do our job for fear of making mistakes.

Part of our God-given role is to correct, to discipline, to set boundaries and call for change. We won't always know exactly what to say or how to say it, and we won't always say it right. But with a heart of love, speak we must.

Some Final Encouragement

God knows you aren't perfect, but according to him, you are still the most important person in the plan. God must have thought we had it in us, or he would have already come up with a better approach or better people to do the job.

Peter tells us that "love covers a multitude of sins" (1 Peter 4:8). You will sin in raising your kids. You will make lots of mistakes in what you say and in what you fail to say. James says that if we never make a mistake in our speech, we are perfect (James 3:2). Only one person ever pulled that off, and that is why he is our Lord, and we are his followers.

You will stumble and fall. Get back up, dust yourself off, and try again. Listen and learn. Speak from your heart and listen to theirs as well. Keep learning and growing, knowing that God will help you and them to connect—soul to soul and heart to heart.

Part 4
Finishing

Chapter 13

A Torrent of Technology

He said to the crowd: "When you see a cloud rising in the west, immediately you say, 'It's going to rain,' and it does. And when the south wind blows, you say, 'It's going to be hot,' and it is. Hypocrites! You know how to interpret the appearance of the earth and the sky. How is it that you don't know how to interpret this present time? Why don't you judge for yourselves what is right?"

Luke 12:54–57

Every generation of parents has to cope with change. The world in which our parents raised us is vastly different from the one we face today. And the pace of change has sped up in recent years. There was only an eleven-year span between our four kids, but Geri and I saw immense differences in the world our youngest and oldest children had to face. The challenges our youngest one encountered, and that we had to deal with in raising her, were more intense, threatening and difficult.

The faster the growth of technology, the more quickly parents have to learn and adapt. If we aren't up to speed with what is going on in the world in which our children live, we will be lost in the fog. And if we are out of touch, our kids will pay the price.

We need to heed the warning given by Jesus in the beginning

passage, in which he chides us for not being aware of what is happening right in front of our faces.

When I Was a Kid...

Let me share with you some of what I saw happen during my growing-up years. Now, before you write me off as hopelessly outdated, realize that your reactions to some of what I am about to share are the same as your own kids' reactions as they try to help you find your way through the maze of technology that to them seems—pardon the expression—child's play.

I grew up in the 1950s. I had three older sisters, all of whom were teens during those amazing years. I got to observe the changes that came into our family during that decade, which was a time of tremendous social and technological change. Parents had to cope with some new phenomena, and to the burgeoning availability of technology that had previously been inaccessible to the average family.

I remember the advent of "car dating." The automobile and its availability increased, and now, teenagers were going out together, all alone, away from the prying eyes of parents. Used to be, a boy came calling, and maybe the young couple sat in the parlor or out on the front porch, or maybe took a walk.

No more! Now, drive-in movies and "going parking" become notorious for the sexual opportunity they provided for unprincipled or naive young men and women.

The telephone morphed into a multi-headed monster. Gone were the days of "party lines" where numerous neighbors shared one line and could thereby pick up and listen in on your conversations.

But then, soon after, there was more. No longer just one telephone unit per house—there were extensions. Kids got their own phones—in their own bedrooms!

And our family got our first television! Now, we no longer

sat around the radio listening to the latest serial program; we viewed a TV screen—at first just black and white with the infamous "rabbit ears" for signal reception. We were lucky; we even had two or three channels to choose from.

And from there, color TV, and multiple sets per home gradually became commonplace for our family and for our society.

I know to some of you this seems hopelessly archaic, but to others of us, the memory of these great advances and changes are vivid memories.

My family stepped into the new era and got an extension phone. We had it mounted on the wall right outside my sisters' bedroom. Wow! This was really big! But, as so often happens with new technology, it brought problems.

My dad became concerned that the girls were talking too much on the phone. (As a little brother, I agreed. The girls were on the phone way too much with their silly girlfriends and especially with their stupid boyfriends.)

It so happened that during this time we had taken in an additional teenage girl, a cousin, who did not respond too well to my dad's insistence on limited phone time.

My dad came up with a solution. I came home from school one day and found my sisters' phone taped up with what must have been an entire roll of packing tape wrapped tightly around it! As a pestering little brother, I thought this was hilarious, but for my teenage sisters, it was a disaster of the first magnitude, caused by a hopelessly outdated and out-of-touch father. None of their friends' dads were so utterly unreasonable and old-fashioned!

As for "car dating," my dad had rules—strict rules—about when the girls had to be home. One night one of my sisters failed to come in on time. As the minutes ticked ominously away, I lay awake in bed, terrified. Knowing my dad's infamous volatile temper, I was not only worrying if my sister had had an accident, but more so for her well-being if she had not.

When the miscreants finally arrived home with a lame excuse, my dad had a non-technological answer: he lifted her date, Billy, off the ground by his shirt collar, pinned him to the wall, and with his nose about two inches away, let him know exactly what he thought about his behavior.

In the 1960s science brought us drugs that were more sophisticated, powerful and available than at any time in history. The avalanche caught most parents completely off guard and unprepared.

In the '70s and '80s we hurtled forward with the CD player, video games and the personal computer. And since that time, technological growth has only progressed faster, with cell phones and the Internet leading the way.

So what are we facing right now? What's going on in your house, in your kids' lives that has you scrambling to know how to respond?

Computers

Computers and the Internet have opened new worlds of power and information to us and our children. Perhaps "breathtaking" is the best word to describe the pace of growth in the power and presence of computers in our homes, and in the lives of our children. But with the blessing has come the curse.

Never in the history of mankind has the availability of pornography been so easy. What used to mean a trip to the store to buy a dirty magazine has now been replaced by the press of a button. One keystroke brings your child into a world of sexual perversion and degradation that can forever leave them scarred and enslaved.

As author R. Kent Hughes says in his book *Set Apart*,[1] the deluge of pornography today is unique in its availability, affordability and anonymity. No money required. No risky trip to the

1. R. Kent Hughes, *Set Apart* (Wheaton: Crossway, 2003).

corner newsstand or minute market. No chance of Mom looking under the mattress or up on the closet shelf for your stash of girlie magazines.

It's just you sitting alone in front of your computer. One stroke of the key and you are seeing heterosexual and homosexual porn, or a combination thereof.

Or, you are seeing perversion like bestiality, sexual domination and violence, and even live sex acts right before your eyes. And, your child is at risk of being contacted by the people behind the scenes who want to take advantage of him or her in any way they can.

We have to understand just how powerful such images are when flashed upon the developing mind of a child or a teenager. Their way of looking at sex, the human body and themselves is forever altered. The images burn into the neural pathways and create not only a perverted picture, but an addictive drive for more.

In preparing a lesson for a parenting seminar, we asked our youngest son, Jonathan, what he would offer as advice for parents. (Since he is still single and in his twenties, he is still somewhat hip and relatable.) He told us that he would most urge parents to guard their sons from Internet pornography. He related that in his experience, many young men of his generation had become first exposed to porn when they were very young, via their home computer or those of friends.

Jonathan observed that many of those young men now have a tremendous problem overcoming the addiction they have developed. And, it has affected their ability to relate to women, and certainly damaged and undermined their confidence and their relationship with God.

Besides the obvious power of pornography, there is the alluring network of chat rooms and easy communication that can ensnare and harm our children. Even the seemingly innocent engines Facebook and MySpace can be dangerous.

Many of us parents are so bewildered by, and unfamiliar with, these entities that we do not have the confidence to respond or to give proper guidance and protection to our kids.

Remember this: it does not matter how sophisticated your knowledge is, you are still in charge, and you are still the parent. While we need to become acquainted with these innovations, the fact that we know less—even far less—than our kids should not undermine our confidence in ourselves or in our God-given role as parents.

Really, the idea of parents being outdated and irrelevant is as old a concept as parenting itself. God has spoken authoritatively about your role whether you know much or little about technology. Your common sense will give you just about all you need to deal with this—if you stay reasonably informed, and if you do not lose your confidence.

Some Suggestions

1. The home computer is in a public place

If we allow a child or a teen to have a secret life in a secluded place on a computer, we are handing them the instrument of their own destruction. Do not be naive. Even a child with innocent intentions can become exposed and addicted to porn—by accident.

So aggressive are the purveyors of sexual sin that they will place it in front of kids without them looking for it. Is this not clearly the work of our great Enemy and Adversary, who is continually on the prowl, looking for a soul to devour?

2. The home computer is technologically protected

There are programs and ways to block the access of porn to your computer. Research the subject. Pay the price for the programs you need to firewall your computer. Monitor your device to be sure that nothing is getting through.

3. You set rules for computer usage

We would not think of allowing a child behind the wheel of a car or to play with dangerous home devices. Why don't we exercise the same common sense when it comes to something of a power just as great? Parents decide when, where and what goes on with the computer. Make the rules. Enforce them. Better too strict than too permissive. Don't doubt yourself. Don't buy the "but everybody else is doing it" line.

4. Parents decide when and if computer privileges such as Facebook and MySpace are allowed

Who says that these programs and their use is a God-given right? Kids are too young to know what is good for them. If you don't think they are ready, then don't let them do it. And if you do grant these privileges, you should unapologetically monitor what your children place on the site, who they speak with, and what they speak about.

Let's elaborate. If and when you do allow these privileges, explain that with privilege comes responsibility. And, not just responsibility, but direction and parental control. From the get-go let your kids know that everything they place on their site, and everything that they receive on it will be seen and approved by you.

I remember looking through the site of one of my kids and seeing a posted photo that I was not comfortable with. There was nothing obviously wrong with the picture, and I am sure the motives of my child were innocent. I just thought that the image it portrayed could be taken in the wrong way. Off it went.

Cell Phones

When my oldest daughter entered college in the mid 1990s, not many of her fellow students had cell phones. By the time she graduated just before the year Y2K, just about everybody did. Sometimes, we don't realize how quickly change is happening and the profound impact it is making.

Previous to the cell phone era, kids had to place a call from a phone in their own home or in a public place like a phone booth (remember those?). And, if they called a friend, many times their friend's parents answered, or at least knew that the phone was in use. And, if parents were really sneaky, they could deftly pick up on the call from an extension somewhere else in the house.

But with the advent of the cell phone, all of that changed. Now, if kids have their own phones, they can make or receive calls anytime, anywhere, and to anybody. The dangers are obvious—or should be.

Not only can our kids waste huge amounts of time in idle chatter; they can be on the phone at the wrong time and with the wrong kinds of people. Even for us adults, the supposedly helpful cell phone can become a tyrannical interrupter of our privacy and of our lives. Unless we set some boundaries, we are never free from its intruding and persistent cry for our attention.

Text messaging adds a whole new dimension. Messages fly back and forth without a word being spoken. Kids are so practiced, skilled and adroit that they can text message from anywhere, at any time. They can do so with a dexterity and rapidity that defies adult imagination. I have seen kids "texting" someone else while (supposedly) engaged in an intense conversation. They hardly break stride.

Just as with the Internet, cell phones have the capacity for the transmission of pictures and images. I am amazed at the massive volume of photos that kids send back and forth. You need to be aware of what kinds of pictures your kids are seeing on their phones. Frequently look through their files. And, let them know that if they receive anything questionable, they need to show it to you.

Some Suggestions

Just as with computers, cell phones are a privilege and not a right. As their affordability has increased, so cell phones have multiplied. What used to be reserved for adults is now the property of all—even the youngest of kids.

While this can be a blessing that enables us to keep in touch with our kids and monitor their safety, the downsides are ominous. At the very least we should set hours when they are off limits. Some examples: family functions, mealtimes, study hours, later evening time. Let your kids know that you will check the monthly bill, and that you can and will go online and monitor their calling and texting records to be sure they are acting responsibly.

If kids are not mature enough to monitor themselves, then parents should not hesitate to take possession of the cell phone during off-limit times. Kids who continually or defiantly abuse cell phones should be relieved of them. A little discipline firmly given and strongly enforced will get great results.

Just as in other areas of life, parents need to teach kids proper etiquette. Taking all but the most important and urgent of calls during a conversation or during other social events needs to be off-limits. Texting during class is obviously out of line. Talking on the phone during family time or in the midst of other more important duties is out of place.

Kids are at risk enough while driving—cell phone usage, both talking and texting, while behind the wheel can be lethal. Are we getting the picture? If we don't teach and enforce some etiquette and norms, bad habits will set in.

TV and Video Games

TV is not a new technology, but the proliferation of TV sets in the home is a relatively new development. Most families have multiple TV sets, and many of us assume that our kids should have their own set in their room. (And could the main reason we allow this be that we don't want any competition with our favorite shows?)

Think again. Most kids just cannot handle it. We must remember the power and influence of what the media is pumping out before we accede to it going into our kids' private rooms. Avoid this, not only for the kinds of things they will see, but because of the sheer amount of time they will waste in front of the set.

Sexually explicit shows now abound, even in the daytime and early evening hours that used to be reserved for "family entertainment." And who defines what that is, anyway? Let's face it: the folks making those decisions do not claim to live by the standards laid out in God's word. Their norms are lower—abysmally lower—than what godly people should accept. And even if a show is okay, the advertisements accompanying it may be outright suggestive and salacious.

Things have gotten so bad that we may need to turn the set off completely, unless we are right there to monitor what is going on. Even sporting events are not immune—professional teams have "cheerleaders" who are more akin to strip club performers, and many of the uniforms and dance moves of the teams of college squads are openly immodest and suggestive.

Video games got their start in the 80s and have become a staple in society now. Children have a whole set of expectations of what games they "ought" to have and be playing.

Video games can be sexual and violent. Many parents are allowing their sons to play games that show explicit violent scenes, with blood, gore, screams and hate-filled language and expressions.

Other games are dark and sinister, creating a world of characters and plots that are evil and degrading. Are we so foolish as to think these images and themes don't adversely affect the minds and emotions of our kids?

Even in the "innocent" days of the 80s, Geri and I saw this happen with our two young sons. They had a video game that featured dual controls and consisted of a fight between two digital foes. Each boy controlled the punches and kicks with his own joy stick.

We thought little of this, but we noticed, in time, that our normally peaceful sons, who usually played well together, were becoming more and more aggressive, surly and pushy. Our friends and babysitters made the same observation. We figured out that the violent game was creating issues that they had never experienced before. We scrapped the game, and with that, the problem went away.

We also saw that our boys were becoming increasingly desirous to spend time playing the other games that we still allowed. We noticed that they got a glazed look on their faces as they sat transfixed before the screen, moving nothing but their fingers and their eyes, totally immersed in what they were doing.

We didn't like what we saw. We decided to limit video games to twenty-minute sessions. And, the same rules applied when they were visiting friends. We let the parents of their friends know of our standards, and asked them to enforce them with our boys when they were visiting in their homes.

We believe that these stands made a huge contribution to the growth and development of our sons, and that they were spared the violent and isolating affects that video games have had on so many boys.

Just as with the cell phone, we need to teach some manners

and establish some boundaries when it comes to video games. Even though it may conveniently keep them occupied, beware of allowing kids to get into their own world of portable games when you are at social gatherings or when you want your family to have time together.

Some Suggestions

Never just put kids in front of the TV, turn it on, and leave them there. Don't let the network make the decision for you—choose for yourself what your children will see. Even though TV can keep the kids quiet and give us some precious free time, we must not let our own convenience win out over what is best for our kids. Instead of being dictated to by the programmers, why don't we select some of the excellent parent-approved videos and play them for our children.

Avoid letting your kids sit and watch TV by default when they have nothing else to do. Don't let them just sit with the remote, paging through the channels. See that they choose an appropriate program to watch. It may even be best for you to view it with them. Geri did this with Alexandra with one of her favorite shows, which, though well-written and witty, had some content that we did not approve of.

Being there alongside our daughter allowed Geri to give her input and observations on the dialogue between the characters and the kinds of decisions they made. Yes, Alexandra groaned a little at first, but it became a cherished mother-daughter event, and ended up being a positive experience.

Block out the channels that you feel are inappropriate. Even the standard home packaging can have explicit and violent programming. We did not allow even the "mature" movie channels into our home, and we never regretted our decision.

Another strategy, especially during summer vacation and on weekends, is to decide that each child gets to select one program of limited duration to watch per day. This prevents our kids' summer holidays and weekends from being dominated by random TV watching.

Parents, all we are trying to say is that we need to be aware and proactive in setting boundaries for our children and television. A little thought and planning goes a long way towards keeping your kids from being addicted to the TV and being harmed by inappropriate programming.

Facing the Technological Torrent

Parents, God has given us a precious and grave responsibility. We are to raise our kids, and not just leave them to their own devices—or to the devices of technology. We are to protect them from the corrosive and toxic influences of the world. While we cannot flee from this world, we must not mindlessly or heedlessly allow it to encroach into our lives. Technology is a wonderful gift, but it can be a source of unspeakable harm.

Don't be naive. And, we repeat—don't lose confidence, just because you are not as technologically savvy as your kids. Morality, right and wrong, good judgment, and godliness are not outmoded by technological advances. These values and standards are eternal.

You are the force God has placed in the lives of your kids to protect and nurture them. Read the signs of the times. See the world for what it is. Resist any incursion of technology that harms your kids—whether it is their minds, their emotions or their actions. Their lives, their future and their souls depend upon it.

Chapter 14

Sex and Dating

Do not be overcome by evil, but overcome evil with good.
Romans 12:21

We live in a sexually confused world. Our children are confronted with temptations that most of us did not have to face until we were much, much older. If there is any realm where they need guidance, this is it. Wherever we are today, we need to start working with our kids in this area and the sooner, the better.

What do our children need in their hearts and characters to overcome the sexual challenges and temptations they will face?

An assured trust in God

> "For I know the plans I have for you," declares the LORD,
> "plans to prosper you and not to harm you, plans to give
> you hope and a future." (Jeremiah 29:11)

Our children must believe that God is good and that whatever he says and does is for their benefit. If God forbids something, he is not just trying to deprive them, and he is not being arbitrary; it is for their good.

Kids must also believe that God knows best. They must trust that God's wisdom is higher than theirs and that he not only is amazingly intelligent, but that he has the sovereign capacity to arrange the specific events of their lives into a beautiful plan. It naturally follows that since marriage is God's will for the vast majority of people (1 Corinthians 7:1–7), then God has someone in mind for them to marry, and he will move heaven and earth to get the two of them together.

Knowing and believing these things about God prevents a sullen resignation or active rebellion against his will. Kids who have a serene, poised trust in God and his good plan for their lives are less likely to allow their passions to lead them into sexual sin or into marrying someone outside God's kingdom. It makes them virtually unfazed by any teasing, ridicule or pressure they may receive for their "strange" high standards from their schoolmates and friends.

I remember when I was still a teenager (age nineteen) and Geri and I were dating, I would from time to time receive unsolicited advice from my college fraternity brothers. They could not understand why Geri and I were not together every waking (and sleeping!) hour. "Someone's going to take her away from you if you don't watch out," they would counsel.

I am sure some of them thought there had to be something wrong with my sexual orientation since Geri and I were not going to bed together. Some of the advice was well-intentioned and some was just plain ridicule. But the fact is, after many years of marriage, Geri and I are still happily in love. God's plan works. And nowhere is that seen any more plainly than in his plan for sex and sexual intimacy.

What I am saying is that we must teach our kids to trust God absolutely. They must trust in the goodness of God's heart, that he only wants the best for them. They must trust in the goodness of his word, especially as it applies to sexual matters. And finally, they must trust in the goodness of God's ways, that if they seek him first, he will orchestrate all the events of their lives to place them with that special someone they can love, cherish and enjoy forever.

A positive view of sex

> So God created man in his own image, in the image of God he created him; male and female he created them. (Genesis 1:27)

> God saw all that he had made, and it was very good. (Genesis 1:31)

Sex is a beautiful creation of God. Sexual attraction and sexual pleasure are intrinsically good. There is nothing evil about the sexual part of our nature. It is something God has placed within us not just to assure the propagation of the next generation, but to give us joy and pleasure in life.

Some of us mistakenly believe that sex is the devil's domain and was the "forbidden fruit" of the Garden of Eden. Maybe we picked this up from weirded-out medieval theology or from the misguided, twisted understanding of holiness we got from our childhood churches, but this attitude is wrong, unhealthy and will lead our children into frustration, guilt and sexual sin.

Don't let sex be taken away from God and turned over to Satan—it is one of God's greatest gifts. Satan has taken this gift and has twisted it for selfish purposes, but sex in itself is a beautiful thing. Don't let your children grow up thinking that all of the people out in the world are really having a great time sexually, but if someone serves God, they never will. It is a lie on both counts.[1]

Teach them that God wants them to have a great sexual life, but at the right time, in the right way, with the right person. This knowledge takes most of the punch right out of sexual temptation. When kids know that sex is good and that God is going to give them a great marriage with a wonderful sexual experience,

---

1. To help you as parents to have a godly view of sex, I suggest my book *The Five Senses of Romantic Love: God's Plan for Exciting Sexual Intimacy in Marriage,* published in 2008 by DPI.

then the attractiveness and appeal of the world's counterfeits lose their power. Our kids are in a battle for a godly understanding of sex. Half the battle is controlling the passions; the other half is realizing that sexual sin is falsely presented by the world.

A reverence for the human body

> It is God's will that you should be sanctified; that you should avoid sexual immorality; that each of you should learn to control his own body in a way that is holy and honorable, not in passionate lust like the heathen, who do not know God; and in this matter no one should wrong his brother or take advantage of him. (1 Thessalonians 4:3–6)

We are created in the image of God. As such, our bodies are honorable, noble and worthy of our highest respect. The body is not an evil thing to be disdained, feared and ashamed of. The term "the flesh" (or "sinful nature" in the NIV) is not equated in the Scriptures with the term "the body." We are to honor God with our bodies (1 Corinthians 6:20). If our bodies are basically evil, then how can we honor God with them? "The flesh" has reference not to our bodies but to those rebellious impulses in us that lead us to warp our legitimate desires to selfish ends. It refers to that part of our nature that longs for independence from God and that wants no control or limitation of its will.

Kids who respect their own bodies and the bodies of others possess a great weapon against sexual sin. Knowing that the human body is honorable and holy enables them to regard the lustful displays in pornography, television, music videos and movies as something degrading. Young people who learn to be abhorred and offended by the flaunting of the human body are not as susceptible to the allure of lust and pornography. When we approach the subject in this way, we put our children on the high ground of righteousness, rather than in a defensive position in which they always are having to fight off temptation. And when they are on the high ground, they are far more likely to win the battle.

A high regard for the body is one of the best ways to help children deal with the temptation of masturbation. When kids understand that the purpose of sex is for the conception of children and for the mutual enjoyment and fulfillment of husband and wife, they realize that masturbation falls outside the purposes of God. They see that sex is meant to be an act of unselfish love between a husband and wife.

It follows then, that to seek sexual fulfillment outside of that relationship is foolish and sinful. Although the Bible does not deal with the subject of masturbation directly, it is my personal conviction that it is wrong, for the above reasons and more. It is virtually always associated with lust; it is enslaving; it creates a selfish attitude toward sex; it offends the conscience, and paralyzes us with guilt. We should urge our children not to become involved in this unhealthy practice.

That having been said, we need to realize that as younger children begin to awaken sexually, they go through a period of self-discovery, and that some degree of bodily exploration may result. They may become quite aware of, and fascinated by, the pleasant sensations that come from touching their sexually sensitive areas. It would be a mistake to overreact to these incidents and treat them as if they were in the same category as those of older children.

However, it is at this time that we need to begin to teach our little ones about their bodies, and the way that God made them. We need to explain that they are "fearfully and wonderfully made" by God (Psalm 139:14), and we ought to help them to have respect—even reverence—for their bodies as the handiwork of their loving Creator.

We can take comfort in knowing that when we approach the subject of sex from a spiritual and biblical point of view, we are standing on solid ground. Teaching our children from a young age that sex is a wonderful gift from God provides an understanding that will strengthen them immensely when the time comes for them to fight the battle for sexual purity.

And, of equal importance, we are building between us an openness and trust that is likely to continue. Having this kind of talking relationship with you can spare your kids the experience of isolation, confusion and shame that is the lot of so many as they enter puberty. Parents, let's keep the doors of communication wide open, and not allow sex to become a realm of conversation into which we and our children cannot enter.

A respect for the opposite sex

> In the Lord, however, woman is not independent of man, nor is man independent of woman. For as woman came from man, so also man is born of woman. But everything comes from God. (1 Corinthians 11:11–12)

Men and women are in adversarial roles more so today than ever before. The gender conflict that used to be amusing or, at most, annoying has in recent years turned downright ugly. Sexual harassment, date rape, inequitable pay scales—these are but a few of the issues that have heightened a conflict that traces its roots back to the Garden of Eden.

The solution to this problem, and to the associated problem of sexual promiscuity, is to teach your children to respect the opposite sex. Help them to value the difference between the genders and not to ridicule or disdain them.

Young boys should not look down upon girls as silly, emotional, fickle weaklings. Teach your boys to respect the intelligence, talents and competence of women in all fields of endeavor and to appreciate and respect their contributions, whenever and wherever they make them.

As boys grow up, they must not come to view women as sex objects, placed at their disposal for the gratification of their lustful desires. Young men should be taught that they are responsible for controlling their own passions. Never let your sons buy into the worldly idea that the burden of saying "no" falls upon the girl alone and that if a girl is "easy," then she deserves to be taken advantage of.

In a like manner, girls must also be taught to respect boys. When girls are young, they must see boys as more than clumsy, insensitive, rude oafs who function at just above cave man level. As they grow older, girls need to appreciate boys' built-in desires to lead, to achieve, and to prove themselves in the competitive male environment. Some in the feminist movement would have us believe that men are basically lustful and exploitative and that women should be perpetually on guard against them, never giving their hearts to any man fully, in order to avoid being hurt or taken advantage of.

Others of this mind-set look at men as basically unfeeling, insensitive, disloyal bums who will walk out on women at a moment's notice. We all know men who are this way and realize that there is some truth in these stereotypes. But it is wrong to allow or encourage our girls to grow up feeling this way about men—if we do, we set them up for a life of misery and conflict.

Teach mutual respect. Model it in your marriage. Then your kids will escape the warped, over-reactive ways of the world. They will have a healthy respect for the opposite gender that will lead them to a joyful marriage and to a peaceful adjustment in life.

A high view of marriage

Marriage should be honored by all. (Hebrews 13:4)

Marriage has fallen on hard times. About half of the people who marry end up divorcing, and many married couples who do stay together are not very happy. It is no surprise then that often marriage is not highly respected. Many critics are actively hostile to marriage, blaming it for our personal and social problems. They look at it as the poorest choice out of many available options to arrange our sexual and personal relationships.

Even in the church, some of us have adopted these kinds of worldly, unbiblical attitudes. We may have suffered through a bad marriage (or two, or three...), or perhaps we have been listening to the worldly voices around us. Whatever the reason, some of us find it hard to wholeheartedly recommend marriage to our children.

We must formulate our convictions from the Scriptures and not by our own failures or by the persuasion of worldly thought. God himself designed marriage—and he did a great job of it. Marriage is not the problem; people are. When we get *us* right, marriage comes out just fine.

The influence of the world here is pervasive. If your kids took a poll in their classrooms, how many children would be from single-parent homes (either by birth to an unmarried mother or by divorce)? Many of their classmates are now with a stepparent. Others are in situations where an unmarried man and woman are living together. Still others are from homes where the marriage is devoid of love and perhaps filled with verbal and physical conflict. And the portrait of family life painted by television, literature and film does little to raise our sights any higher.

We must counteract this with the positive biblical teaching that marriage is a beautiful relationship, designed by God for our happiness and as the proper environment in which to raise children.

Our children must know that marriage, in spite of its difficulties, is from God and is a glorious thing. Let them know that the years of courtship are just that—years to let God lead them to the right person. Teach them that the privileges of sexual intimacy and of living under the same roof are reserved for people who are married in the eyes of God and according to the laws of the land. Let us encourage our children to look forward to their engagement and wedding days as two of the greatest days of their lives. And let us model for them a noble and romantic view of marriage that they unashamedly uphold, not only for themselves, but for others.

If we deeply believe these things and teach them faithfully to our kids, we are preparing them to fulfill in their lives the dream of a wonderful marriage.

A commitment to date and marry within the church

> Do not be yoked together with unbelievers. For what do righteousness and wickedness have in common? Or what fellowship can light have with darkness? (2 Corinthians 6:14)

> ...she is free to marry anyone she wishes, but he must belong to the Lord. (1 Corinthians 7:39)

Marriage to those outside God's kingdom always has been disapproved by God (Nehemiah 13:27) and has inevitably had disastrous consequences for God's people (1 Kings 1:1-2). It is my own solid conviction that it is wrong for a disciple of Jesus to marry someone who is not also a disciple. It is also my conviction that since dating is the usual cultural means by which we in this day and time select a marriage partner, then our children should date only within the family of God, the church.

These are heart-convictions that we must impart to our children early in life. In some ways, it naturally attaches itself to all else we believe. If we want to devote our lives to loving God with all of our heart, soul, mind and strength, it stands to reason that we would want to spend the rest of our lives with someone who shares that same conviction with us.

232

What do we do when our children are attracted to someone at school who is interested in them and is a reasonably nice person? We taught our children that while it was fine to be friends with kids like this, they must not become romantically involved. We didn't want our children to withdraw from others, but our kids knew without question how Geri and I felt about them going out with someone like this—it was strictly off-limits.

When our daughters were in high school, they would sometimes get asked out by boys at school. They learned to give a pleasant, routine explanation that they very much appreciated the invitation, but that they chose to go out only with guys from their church because of their desire to be united spiritually with whomever they dated. They were careful not to make it a personal rejection, nor to come across self-righteously. They also offered an invitation to their friends to come with them to church or to teen activities.

I would urge all of us to put these convictions deep within our children's souls. If we do this, we vastly increase the odds that their hearts will not be pulled away from God because they get emotionally involved with someone outside his kingdom.

If we teach this and lay a carefully reasoned foundation of conviction beneath it, we are helping to ensure that our children marry wonderful Christians who will be a blessing not only to them, but to us as well.

An understanding of the nature of sexual temptation

> Put to death, therefore, whatever belongs to your earthly nature: sexual immorality, impurity, lust, evil desires.
> (Colossians 3:5)

Sexual attraction and temptation are the most powerful forces your children will have to grapple with as they enter into maturity. Problems arise not only from desires within themselves but from a world that flaunts sex before children at younger and younger ages. We must provide our children with the biblical teaching and advice they will need to successfully find their way down this difficult path.

In tackling the issue of lust, we need to understand what lust is, and what it is not. Let us go through this step by step together.

(1) Sexual attraction is not necessarily sin. Seeing a girl or boy and thinking they are cute, beautiful or handsome is not wrong. It is quite normal. If kids equate sexual attraction to sexual lust, they will be tormented by guilt and frustrated by the impossibility of overcoming their God-given impulses. Some kids with extremely sensitive consciences will need plenty of help here.

(2) Sexual lust occurs when your child crosses the line from attraction to arousal. More specifically, lust occurs when:
- they continue to look at something explicitly sexual.
- they look at someone for the purpose of desiring them sexually.
- they engage in fantasies involving sexual images or sexual activity.

(3) Sexual lust does not occur just because any of the following things happen to your child:
- their heart skips a beat when someone they like walks up.
- they notice an attractive girl or a cute boy.
- they struggle with the urge to look at a pornographic magazine or video.
- something comes before their eyes that will incite lust, but they quickly look away.
- a sexual thought passes through their minds.
- their body has a physical sexual response—even when they are not focused on sexual things. Parents, it is here that we will need to do some extensive and sensitive teaching to help our children as they mature sexually. As a part of this

process they will experience emotional and physical sensations which are both powerful and difficult for them to understand. It is important for you to help them through this time, and into an appreciation and respect for the way God has created them.

(4) We must help our kids discern the difference between the list in number 2 and the list in number 3. Some kids are so sensitive in conscience that they equate temptation with lust. Not so! We know Jesus was tempted to lust because the Bible says he was tempted in every way we are (Hebrews 4:15). Don't let Satan throw your children into pits of self-accusation simply because they have to fight off evil thoughts.

Other kids who have very little conscience will deceive themselves into thinking everything is fine, when it is not. Kids like this will flirt with lust and end up getting trapped by it because they are not heeding the Bible's teaching to "flee from sexual immorality" (1 Corinthians 6:18).

(5) All children need to be taught to have a sober fear of sexual lust and of sexual sin and to stay far away from them. This includes guarding their hearts (Proverbs 4:23), their eyes (Proverbs 4:25) and the pathway of their feet (Proverbs 5:8). If they do fall in any way, pray to God that they tell you immediately or that you find out quickly. Sexual sin must be repented of before it has opportunity to gain a serious foothold in our children's lives.

(6) Be very careful with television, the Internet and videos (see chapter 13 for a discussion of this problem).

(7) Help children work through any thoughts that are deviant, abnormal or weird. Some kids have active imaginations, and their minds may wander into some very strange territory. If they talk to you about things like this, listen carefully. Ask enough questions to get the full picture. Don't overreact. Usually just being able to talk about it goes a long way towards solving the problem for a youngster. After you hear everything, give them

any guidance they may need to clear their minds of the unwholesome thoughts.

(8) The best defense is a good offense. A mind can only think one thing at a time. Teach your kids to not only get rid of sinful thinking but to also fill their minds with pure thoughts (Colossians 3:1-4, Romans 8:1-17, Philippians 4:8-9). If they focus on serving God, reading their Bibles, praying and serving others, they will less likely be dragged into sin.

An open door to talk

> ...speaking the truth in love, we will in all things grow up....
> (Ephesians 4:15)

We have already made the point that the lines of communication must be completely open between our kids and us. In no area is it any more important than in sexual matters. As we said in the last section, we should always encourage them to talk to us about sexual issues, and we should listen carefully when they do.

When do we teach our kids about sex and how? I will give a few pointers here:

(1) Don't be afraid to talk about sexuality with your children at a fairly young age. Even in preschool they may hear talk from playmates or see programs on TV about which they need to ask us. Help them to know what behavior is acceptable. Teach them about the private parts of their bodies that others should not touch, and that they should not touch on others.

(2) The time for the "birds and the bees" talk is in elementary school. It is usually best for Mom to talk with the girls and Dad to talk with the boys. It usually needs to happen somewhere between eight and ten, depending on a child's maturity level.[2]

I was really nervous when the time came for me to have "the

---

2. I will not go into detail in this book on how to have "the talk" except to say that when we do we should speak positively, forthrightly and comfortably. See the Bibliography (Recommended Reading) for some helpful resources.

talk" with my oldest son, David. No one ever had "the talk" with me when I was growing up, so I had nothing to go on. I tried to figure out a way to use the Bible to help me. "Why not begin at the beginning?" I thought. So, we opened the Bible to Genesis 1. We read about the creation of the world and of man and woman, and I said, "Son, what do you think it means when God tells them to be fruitful and increase in number?" I was so impressed with my brilliance at using this approach that I got caught completely flat-footed by David's reply. He looked at me very excitedly and said, "Oh, that's when we have lots of conversions and the church grows real fast." Oh yes, the true son of a preacher-man!

A willingness to be guided

> Listen, my son to your father's instruction and
>   do not forsake your mother's teaching.
> They will be a garland to grace your head
>   and a chain to adorn your neck. (Proverbs 1:8–9)

Our kids need to let us guide them as they enter into the years of dating and courtship. They are too young and inexperienced to know what is best. Stubborn, arrogant children who think they are wise enough to run their own lives are sadly mistaken. If they do not change their attitudes and become learners, they will suffer heartbreak of immense proportions. Parents, we must put a learner's heart into our children, especially when it comes to sex and dating.

Let me share with you some of the practical guidance Geri and I have given our children on dating matters.

We didn't mind our elementary and middle-school-age kids having special friends at church of the opposite sex. There were two requirements: they had to keep it on a casual basis, and the relationship had to be spiritually encouraging. Our boys both

237

had girls in the church that they "liked" and who liked them back. They gave each other small gifts and kept up with each other when they were out of town and even talked occasionally on the phone. We considered this to be positive and healthy. But we did not allow them to "go steady" or say they loved each other as some of the kids at their school did—they were just too young. If they ever got any questions about it from their friends, we told them to blame it on us: "My parents say I am too young to go steady right now." It worked like a charm.

We let our kids go out on their first "date" in middle school. In Elizabeth's case, she met one of the boys at a church party and they (sort of) spent the evening together there. We brought her there and took her home. This is the way to start your kids dating: low key, many other people around, and no riding anywhere together without adults in the car.

As kids grow older, you may begin to allow them to go out on "car dates." You need to know that their dates are responsible, trustworthy young men or women from church, and you need to know and approve every aspect of the plan. They don't need to go out for a lengthy time, and they need to be in early. You need to know exactly where your kids are going, and it ought to be a double-date or group date situation, and you need to approve of the other couple(s) on the date.

Gradually give your kids more freedom as they mature, and as they earn trust by their responsible behavior. Teens should demonstrate a great attitude, be communicative, want to do the right thing, and be receptive to your guidance. Freedom and trust in dating, as in other areas, must be earned, and not demanded.

Some of us may be new to all of this, and so are our kids. If your kids are older, you will need to sit down and have a talk before you jump in and start changing things. Teach them the basics and background in the Scriptures first. Give reasonable explanations for your policies. Listen to their questions and work with them to come out in agreement. It is more of a challenge to change bad habits than it is to set up good ones from the outset. But, even if you are getting started late, do all you can to make up for lost time by giving your children the advice they so desperately need.

A joyful life in God's kingdom

The joy of the LORD is your strength. (Nehemiah 8:10)

A joyful, fulfilling life is one of the greatest safeguards available to protect our children from sexual sin. If their lives are full of happiness, then there is far less inclination for kids to go looking in the wrong places for fulfillment. Young people who are having fun in God's kingdom are far less likely to desire the bad things of the world.

Joyful lives for our children must start in our own households. How many kids have become more attracted to sin because they experienced only misery, anger and quarreling in their homes? We simply must build happy families. If there is closeness among all the brothers and sisters and if the whole family has great, joyful times together, then children will be much more likely to strive to live in such a way as to earn their family's respect and approval.

Second, we must model loving, warm relationships as husbands and wives. When our kids admire our marriages, they will be all the more eager to imitate us and listen to our advice about sex and dating.

Our children also need to be a part of an exciting, spiritual ministry for kids in the church. They need to have friends their own ages who are godly, wholesome and fun. Youngsters who are surrounded by peers at church whom they respect, enjoy being with and can readily talk to are much less likely to be drawn away from God to seek fulfillment and approval from worldly companions.

Pitch in and help make the kids' ministry at your church, from the nursery to high school, the best it can be. Get behind it, get involved, get to know the teachers and the other parents. Encourage your kids to be a part of the activities. Give rides, offer to host events in your home, shell out the necessary money, go the second mile—do whatever it takes to help put together a great work for the kids.

One thing we especially encourage is the sending of our kids to the church-sponsored camps, retreats and seminars that are available around the country. In just a few short days, these special events can do more than we can imagine to encourage our children to stay faithful and pure. When kids see so many others from God's kingdom all together in one place, they realize they are part of the hottest thing going on Planet Earth.

It gives a tremendous boost to their spirits and a great incentive to never compromise their sexual standards. Another benefit is that they will make some friends that they can write, call, email and keep up with long afterwards. If some of these new acquaintances are from the opposite gender, this will go very far toward giving our kids the hope and confidence that they will one day find and marry the most awesome person in the world.

Nowhere are the times in which we live more challenging than in the area of sex and dating. We must be confident in God and God's word if we are to raise our children with convictions in this crucial area. Inspire your kids with your life and with your own marriage. Pray for wisdom. Teach them, explain to them, and reason with them. If we build our children's lives on the foundation of God's word and wisdom, they will be protected from the pitfalls and heartache of sexual sin, and will grow up to build strong marriages and families of their own.

My son, if you accept my words
   and store up my commands within you,
turning your ear to wisdom
   and applying your heart to understanding,
and if you call out for insight
   and cry aloud for understanding,
and if you look for it as for silver
   and search for it as for hidden treasure,
then you will understand the fear of the LORD
   and find the knowledge of God.
For the LORD gives wisdom,
   and from his mouth come knowledge and understanding.
He holds victory in store for the upright,
   he is a shield to those whose walk is blameless,
for he guards the course of the just
   and protects the way of his faithful ones.
Then you will understand what is right and just
   and fair—every good path.
For wisdom will enter your heart,
   and knowledge will be pleasant to your soul.
(Proverbs 2:1–10)

Chapter 15

Special Life Situations

God sets the lonely in families.

Psalm 68:6

We will now address two situations that require special attention: single-parent families and composite families.

Single-Parent Families

The statistics tell the story—the number of single-parent households is skyrocketing. More and more people are having to cope with this very challenging family situation. It is difficult enough to raise children when there are two people available to handle the emotional, physical and spiritual stresses. How much more formidable to face them alone!

We now will examine several of the obstacles that single parents must confront and overcome.

Loneliness

The burdens of parenthood are heavy, and without a spouse to help share the emotional load, loneliness can become a debilitating problem. Children are wonderful companions, but they are young and dependent and cannot understand all the feelings we experience as adults. Add to this the fact that divorce or death could be the reason for singleness, and the feelings of loneliness can become overwhelming.

The same is true for mothers who were not married to the fathers of their children. Perhaps you were counting on marriage but were left by yourself to raise the child (or children) alone. The pain, anger and hurt can weigh you down with a depressing, empty feeling of despair, with little hope for change.

So it is for those without God. But for those of you who belong to him, how different your life and your attitude can be! I am reminded of a great statement about God from one of the prophets:

> "For your Maker is your husband—
>   the LORD Almighty is his name—
> the Holy One of Israel is your Redeemer;
>   he is called the God of all the earth." (Isaiah 54:5)

I believe that God, in a unique sense, becomes the husband of single mothers who have committed their lives to him. The passage above refers to God's relationship with his people Israel, but it certainly would refer to individuals also. How encouraging to a single woman to know that God himself takes on the role of husband, since there is no man in the house. Now tell me, is there a better husband available than this one?

Whether you are a single mother or single father, God cares about you. He feels for you and will be with you in a special way to meet your needs. As he cared for the rejected Hagar and her son Ishmael (Genesis 21:17–21), he will wrap his arms of protection around you and your family. God understands loneliness—he once gave up a son. The Lord himself will comfort you through his Spirit when your prayers of anguish are beyond expression (Romans 8:26–27).

But you also have another resource—the family of God, the

church. God sets the lonely in families; and when you were born again to become God's child, you became a member of his great household.

I urge you, become a functional part of the church. Don't let yourself withdraw in frustration and independence. Learn to express your needs to others—they cannot help you if they do not know your needs. And many times, unless people have been there themselves, they will not fully grasp all that you feel. Don't let this become a stumbling block to you. Open your heart and reveal your needs to others, all the while doing your best to avoid a complaining spirit, and you will most likely find yourself surrounded by people who want to help.

Another step I would urge you to take is to develop a close relationship with a spiritually strong two-parent family in your church. Find a family with an excellent mother and father who can be special friends to you and who want to help care for your children. Encourage your kids to be close to theirs. Work to make the relationship between your families so close that you feel entirely comfortable with your children sleeping over at each other's houses.

You also want these two parents to feel free to help you with the discipline and training of your kids. These people cannot pay your bills or live your life for you, but they can lighten your load, increase your joy, and give you a wonderful sense of security.

Build a family life. Even if there are only two of you, you are a family! Think of yourself as a family member first and a single person second. The chapters in this book entitled "Foundations of a Spiritual Family" (chapter 9) and "A Close Family" (chapter 10) are written for you, too. Have meals together. Start your own family traditions. Have family devotionals. Rejoice together and enjoy the family you have.

Discouragement and self-pity

If you do not guard your heart carefully, the loneliness and hurt you feel can turn into discouragement or even self-pity. Discouragement is hard enough to cope with, but self-pity is especially damaging. It is that feeling of "Poor me, no one understands how hard this is. No one appreciates the struggles I have, and why is this happening to me, anyway?"

Self-pity is dangerous because it seems so innocent and is so understandable. But if you let it go unchecked, it will destroy your soul. As we consider the life and example of Jesus, we can take heart knowing that he faced the same emotions we do. He bore the pressures of life without a companion who truly understood and sympathized with him. He understands, and can comfort you in those times when you feel most discouraged.

We must stop dwelling on what might have been and begin to believe that God has a better plan. Realize that everyone has problems, including married people. As great as marriages are meant to be, many of them are hell on earth.

Would you change places with someone in a bad marriage? Life is not easy for anyone. And remember, trials and difficulties are what God uses in all our lives to make us stronger people.

As you deal with your own emotions, you must realize that your children need you to be strong. If you are too open with your tears, hurts and feelings in front of them, they may become insecure and anxious.

You can let them know that you are hurting at times, but do so in a state of emotional self-control. Pour out your tears and anguish to God and to friends in the church. But please, guard your children from coming to believe that you are falling completely apart or that they need to assume the role of parent and take care of you.

You must resist the "I just can't take it any more" attitude. God says, "Yes, you can!" He also says that he will not let you go through anything that inevitably will destroy you (1 Corinthians 10:13). Fill your mind with the promises of God. Whatever the challenge, be it emotional, financial or spiritual, God will be there for you. Trust in God, get to work, and you will find that there is a solution to every problem.

Compromise

The loneliness and strain of raising a child or children by ourselves can leave us emotionally and spiritually vulnerable—so much so that when someone comes along and shows us some attention, we can compromise our convictions and our purity. A sexual surrender may seem like a way to comfort ourselves in our loneliness, but it only leads to despair. Sex outside of marriage is not only sinful, but unrewarding and empty.

As we have already discussed, even if we have scriptural grounds to remarry, we can only marry someone who is a true Christian (1 Corinthians 7:39). We have seen single parents compromise and marry outside the faith, hoping for a good outcome, but any departure from the lordship of Christ always leads to disaster. Even marriage to other Christians, when children are involved, is a daunting challenge.

Remember, you are not just getting married; you are bringing your children into a radically different life. The older they are, the more difficult it will be.

If you are considering marriage, employ great patience and wisdom. It is better to err on the side of caution than to be over-bold. A relationship that seems to feel right still needs to be subjected to the test of time.[1]

This is a difficult and delicate subject, far beyond the scope of this book. But, let us as single parents seek God's guidance as

---

1. See the appendix of *Friends and Lovers* (Spring Hill, TN: DPI, 1996), 173–181, for a more complete discussion of how to evaluate a dating relationship from a spiritual perspective.

we consider the decisions we make, and make them with a sober and settled mind.

Guilt

Some of you are single parents because of sexual sin. Others of you are divorced. You struggle with the reality that your own weaknesses or mistakes were a part of the reason that the marriage did not work. The shame, guilt and sense of failure can be absolutely crushing.

Guilt feelings can make you reluctant to discipline your kids. You feel responsible for your children being in a single-parent home, and to make up for this you try to indulge their every whim. You also may find that you lash out at the children in anger and frustration, only to be seized later with bitter remorse.

I urge you to read great passages in the Bible like Psalm 38, 51 and 103, and scriptures such as Ephesians 1–3 which describe the completeness of your forgiveness in Christ. God does not treat us as our sins deserve. He is slow to anger and full of compassion. He completely forgives and forgets. Don't live in regret.

Many of the greatest characters in the Bible made terrible mistakes, but when they turned back to him, God forgave, and used them in a mighty way. You cannot go back and change what you have done—that is why Jesus died for you. Accept God's grace; let him help you deal with the consequences of your sins and mistakes, and press forward to live a great life!

Being overwhelmed

You are going to have to do several things to cope with the challenges of your schedule, finances and job:

(1) Become disciplined in the use of your time. You will have precious little to waste! Plan out your days. Get your family on a regular schedule. You cannot live as if you have no children.

247

They need regular feeding times, meal times, etc., in their schedules and so do you. Also, spread the work load around by giving the kids regular jobs around the house.

(2) Be solution-oriented. Rely on God and tough out those situations you cannot change. But if you can improve your job, schedule, transportation or finances, then do it.

(3) Get advice. Seek out wise people who can give you ideas on how to improve your career and who can help you become a more marketable employee. Others can help you in setting up a budget and managing your money. Single mothers and fathers, go to other parents in the church for guidance on how you can do a better job raising your kids. If you are surrounded by other singles, it is critical that you find some experienced parents to help advise you on any difficult child-rearing challenges.

(4) Take some breaks. Find some trustworthy friends or family to whom you can entrust your kids, and take an occasional vacation. Kick back, have a blast, sleep in, and do what you love to do. Even a day or two away will have a marvelously refreshing effect. You will come back better equipped to be a good parent. Take care of yourself—your kids will thank you!

Discipline problems with the children

Read the chapters in this book on discipline, obedience, etc., and put them into practice. Don't think that your children have to grow up to be spoiled, disrespectful and unruly just because they have only one parent. Be cool, calm and consistent. Be strong with your kids. God will give you the strength to raise them right. And one other note: if you live with other singles, remember, a kid can handle only one mother or father, and you are it! Certainly your roommates can help, but they aren't meant to carry out your role.

In closing our thoughts for single parents, I want to remind you of some important facts. Have you ever realized that the great prophet Samuel was reared in a single-parent home? Have you ever thought that young Timothy was primarily influenced by his mother and grandmother? Have you ever wondered at what age Joseph died, leaving Mary, Jesus and the rest of the family without a father?

Whatever the answers to these questions, we know this: God, in his sovereign love and power, is always working everything out for our good. He has a great plan for you and for your family. Trust God, never give up, and God will pour out his richest blessings and favor upon you and your family.

Composite Families

By this term, I refer to households that are composed of a mixture of people from different families. In a blended family like this, there is a parent who is not the biological parent of one or more of the children, and there may be children from other parents as well.

These can be very difficult situations. Any time we put together people whose backgrounds, emotions and habits are from differenet roots, there will be crossed wires and difficult adjustments. Some of these marriages don't survive because the children do not adjust to the new spouse and vice versa. If there is a combination of children, there can be envy and competition among them that causes tension and that can pry parents apart.

What can you do to make a family like this work?

Build spiritual unity

> For he himself is our peace, who has made the two one and has destroyed the barrier, the dividing wall of hostility, by abolishing in his flesh the law with its commandments and regulations. His purpose was to create in himself one new man out of the two, thus making peace, and in this one

body to reconcile both of them to God through the cross, by which he put to death their hostility. He came and preached peace to you who were far away and peace to those who were near. For through him we both have access to the Father by one Spirit.

Consequently, you are no longer foreigners and aliens, but fellow citizens with God's people and members of God's household. (Ephesians 2:14–19)

Jesus Christ is the means of building unity in a composite family. (When you think about it, that's exactly what his church is.) If the parents are dedicated to Jesus, and if the children are taught to respect and honor him also, then everyone can come together and put aside personal feelings and preferences for the sake of Christ. It may seem simple, but unity in any situation is possible only through Christ. The challenges of a composite family only highlight the need for Jesus and make it more obvious.

Composite families need to have a very strong regularity and focus in their family devotionals. Singing, praying, studying the Bible together—all of these things help to draw everyone close beneath the fatherly love of God. I also would suggest that such families, especially those with older children, have weekly open family meetings to air out feelings. But, the rule is this: anybody can say anything on his or her mind, *as long as they express it respectfully*. This kind of meeting will go a long way toward forging unity in your home.

Parents must be unified

When you married each other, your commitment was, and still is, to be united for life. You must therefore live that way and hammer out unity with your new spouse on every issue that could possibly divide you.

A composite family is formed after our habits and life patterns are already established. You have a set way of going about things, and habits don't change easily. They are reinforced by memories of the way things used to be—memories that we cling to either out of love or out of a desire for stability.

Parents, you will have to be the examples of the give and take that will be necessary. You will have to have many talks to work things out, and a great spirit of love and compromise will have to rule in your hearts.

Work out how the children will be disciplined. The new parent is going to have to be respected and to have some authority. It may not be exactly the same as if they were the biological parent, but they must have a role of leadership. If the "real" parent is protective and possessive, the new parent will have a hard time being accepted.

Geri and I worked with one situation in which there was a rebellious son who was selfish and obstinate and gave his mother extreme difficulty. After her marriage, when he would behave rebelliously, the new husband would try to step in. Even though the mother was being horribly treated by the son, she would immediately rush to his defense and undercut her husband's efforts to discipline him. Although we tried to get the husband and wife to unite to help the young man, they never really listened. Sadly, the family fell apart, and the husband and wife eventually divorced.

Don't let this happen to you! Work hard to hammer out unity. Talk through your differences in child rearing. Sit down together and study what the Scriptures have to say on parenting. Get competent, godly people to help you come up with wise solutions to any thorny problems. Pray. Make use of all the resources God has made available to help you create a harmonious family.

Win the hearts of the children

If you are the new spouse stepping into an existing family,

you have your work cut out for you. You need to prepare yourself to give plenty of love, and you must be very patient. You are not only marrying a spouse; you are adopting a family. They come as one package; therefore you must love and care for the children.

If the children are young or if they only have a relationship with one of their parents, it can make your job easier. But if the children are older or if the parent was taken away by death or divorce, you must realize that it will require immense amounts of love, understanding and prayer for you to work out a relationship. They are immature and are being tossed by currents of emotion that neither they nor you entirely understand. Love them, give them time, and pray for God to move.

If you are a man coming into a family that has older children, you need to be very patient. You must realize that you cannot step in and immediately be the heavy-handed disciplinarian. You probably will see many behavior problems that need a father's firmness, but you must proceed slowly. Give the children time to know and love you before you take on that role. And understand, with some of the older kids, you never will be able to treat them as if you had raised them from infancy.

You cannot force your way into their hearts. They will have to open the door and let you in. Some of you try to kick the door down. Others bang on the door, waiting impatiently for it to open. Others of you are angry that there is a door there at all and waste your time wishing it would go away. And finally, there are those of you who sit out on the front steps upset and discouraged because you aren't being treated better. Please understand: I am not trying to be hard on you here, but only to appeal to you to remember that this is a decision you made, and to encourage you to take full responsibility for it.

I would urge you to imitate God in his way of winning hearts. When we rejected him, God did not stop loving us. Instead, he loved us sacrificially and gave us his son—his very best. He patiently waited for our response and never gave up, always hoping that one day we would come to trust in his love and give him our hearts. I am not saying that you should become a doormat or that you should allow yourself to be disrespected or disdained. Not at all. But, if God has been so loving and patient with us, can we not do the same for our newly acquired family?

You must not try to replace the individual they have lost. In a strange way, even if the children love you, they may be reluctant to give you their hearts because they may feel in doing so they are being disloyal to their lost parent. The ties of children to their parents run deep. Even if the children have been terribly abused by the now-absent parents, they still have an almost mystical attachment to them. Do not try to destroy or undermine that love. Give them your own love and gradually they can learn to love you both.

I know there is much more to say in these areas than I have been able to cover in a few pages. I certainly hope that the thoughts in this chapter help you in some way if you find yourself in either of these situations.

In the next chapter, we turn to the most important thing that any of us could hope for our children—that they become disciples of Jesus Christ.

Chapter 16

Conversion

"Why were you searching for me?" he asked. "Didn't you know I had to be in my Father's house?"

Luke 2:49

In one sense, the conversions of young people are the same as those who are older. They read the same Bible, believe in the same God, repent of the same sins, and follow the same Lord. But what at first glance seems a simple matter is complicated by the very issue of youth.

How much can they understand? How much do they have to understand? When are they old enough? How much of the world must they experience beforehand? How can we be sure they are making their decisions for the right reasons? Who should be involved in helping them? All these questions, and others like them, mean that we need to look at this subject in greater detail.

Seeing the need for God

Why should I follow Jesus? *Why* should I become a Christian? These are the questions our kids are asking themselves. We may not see that it is these most obvious questions that our children are asking. We, and our kids, may be focused on the actual decision to become a Christian, and the need to make a commitment, rather than the more profound issue of motivation and desire.

Remember, when Jesus issued the call to discipleship, he started with the phrase, "If anyone would come after me..." (Mark 8:34). The word translated "would" can be accurately translated "wishes" or "desires." Thus, the phrase may be rendered, "If anyone *desires* to come after me..." It follows that in order to make a decision to follow Christ, young people must first have a *sincere desire* to do so. If we or they begin with the issues of commitment and discipleship, we are getting ahead of ourselves.

Let's compare this to the idea of marriage. Granted, this will be an imperfect comparison, but perhaps it will help us grasp how our kids need to come to perceive *why* they would make the decision to become Christians. Suppose we said to our teenager: "One day you will get married. This is very important. It is a huge decision. When you get married, you dedicate your whole life to be with one person forever. How about it? Are you ready to commit?"

Whoa! Wrong beginning! Instead, let's start this way: "One day, you will meet someone whom you come to love with all your heart. You will realize that apart from them your life will be incomplete, but that with them, you will be fulfilled, and will become all you were meant to be, and you will be a blessing to them as well. When you meet and come to love that person, you will want to make a decision to give them your love and your heart."

Are we beginning to understand the point? Our teens must be motivated by who calls them to follow, more than just the call to commitment. Our greatest need is to be loved and to love. Only God, who is love, can ultimately meet that need. Even the need to be forgiven is superseded by this. Forgiveness gives us pardon, but that is only so that we can have a relationship with

God. Yes, teens need to see their sins and be grieved by them—profoundly so—but our sins separate us from God, and that is the real problem.

The haunting loneliness that teens try to fill up with sinful pleasures (or friendships, or possessions, etc.) can only be filled by God. As Jesus said to the Samaritan woman,

> "Everyone who drinks this water will be thirsty again, but whoever drinks the water I give him will never thirst. Indeed, the water I give him will become in him a spring of water welling up to eternal life." (John 4:13–14)

When your teen sees this need, the need that God alone can meet, then the greatest issue in conversion—the *why*—has been resolved.

We as parents cannot make our kids see their need, but we can help them see it. We can even share how we came to see it for ourselves. What can we do? We can *enlighten* them by sharing God's word and our own experience, we can *inspire* them by our faith, and we can *encourage* them as they see our heart.

Making the decision

> Then he called the crowd to him along with his disciples and said: "If anyone would come after me, he must deny himself and take up his cross and follow me. For whoever wants to save his life will lose it, but whoever loses his life for me and for the gospel will save it. What good is it for a man to gain the whole world, yet forfeit his soul? Or what can a man give in exchange for his soul? If anyone is ashamed of me and my words in this adulterous and sinful generation, the Son of Man will be ashamed of him when he comes in his Father's glory with the holy angels." (Mark 8:34–38)

In the passage above Jesus sets forth the basic elements involved in the decision to become his disciple.

(1) A deep desire. As we have been explaining, it all starts with "wishes" or "desires." In order to have a valid conversion experience, young people must have a sincere desire to follow Christ that arises from within their own hearts.

(2) A genuine faith. To entrust their life to Jesus, our kids will have to come to trust him completely. Being raised in a Christian home does not mean that our kids will never have doubts about God, about whether Jesus is God's son, or whether the Bible is God's word. In our case, each one of our kids struggled with some form of doubt as they wrestled with the decision to follow Christ.

When this happened, Geri and I were actually relieved to know they were thinking for themselves and not just coasting on our faith. When those doubts come to your kids, don't panic, and don't be afraid. Point them to some resources to help them answer their questions, and share how you faced and overcame your own doubts. They will come out with a faith that is tested and that is truly their own.

(3) A denial of self. The requirement of Jesus is that "he must deny himself" (v34). Fundamental to the idea of conversion is the concept of self-denial. The "self" is defined simply as your true inner person, the real "you."

Unless teens see themselves for who they are apart from God, they cannot be converted. How can they deny themselves if they have never seen or faced themselves? Young people must grasp how they express their rebellion against God and who they will become apart from his controlling influence.

Once they have seen this, they are now able to truly decide that they will "no longer live for themselves but for him who died for them" (2 Corinthians 5:15).

257

(4) A crucified life. Jesus challenges every follower to "take up his cross" (v34). What does this mean? In short, it indicates that we must die to ourselves (Galatians 2:20), to the world (Galatians 6:14) and to sin (Colossians 3:5–11). We discussed the concept of dying to ourselves in the previous section. What about the other two things to which we must die, "the world" and "sin"?

"The world" has reference to the entire system of people and powers who are not yielded to God (1 John 2:15–17, Ephesians 2:1–3). Teens considering the call to discipleship must take a hard look at the world and what it stands for before they can make a real decision. They do not have to go out and experience everything the world has to offer, but they must see in general terms what the world outside the confines of their family and teen group at church is all about.

The concept of "sin" is much easier to deal with since there are such clear definitions and descriptions of it in the Bible. Young people must see the sins they have committed in action, in attitude and by omission. There must be a realization that their sins have offended and hurt God, and must be decisively forsaken. And when sin later tries to reassert itself in the form of temptation, it must be crucified once again (Luke 9:23).

(5) A committed life. Jesus calls for his disciples to follow him (v34). This is the essence of discipleship—an absolute commitment to follow, obey and become like Christ. Young people must realize that this is the greatest decision they will ever make and that it is for life. When they see the seriousness of the calling, combined with greatness of the One who calls, they are equipped to make a proper decision.

(6) A proclaiming life. Jesus says that we cannot be ashamed of his words (v38). When he called his original disciples, be bade them to become "fishers of men" (Mark 1:17). The notion of being sent on a mission, of having a great purpose to share the good news and help others become disciples is woven into the very fabric of being like Christ.

Teens must also prepare themselves for any opposition, criticism or persecution they may receive as a result of sharing their faith.

Maturity

The question arises, "How can we know if our children are mature enough to make this decision?" Let me help by asking several questions of my own. (Note that they correspond with the section immediately previous to this one.)

(1) Are your children mature enough to make a decision about the general direction their lives will take?

(2) Do they understand who they are and who they will become apart from God? Are they ready to deny the rule of self in their lives?

(3) Have they faced up to the sins they have committed? Are they ready to crucify the sins that will continue to tempt them after they become disciples?

(4) Are they ready to follow Jesus? Do they love and admire him? Do they understand the seriousness and totality of the decision?

(5) Are they ready to stand with Christ and be his witness? Do they see that because of following Jesus they will receive opposition and persecution, and that they will be disliked by some people?

These questions are not intended to be a checklist that we scan, looking for the "right" answers. Instead, they are meant to help us to gauge our children's capacities to think in more mature terms. Kids do not have to be adults before they can be converted to Christ. They must, however, have progressed beyond the stage of innocent childhood and be able to wrestle with the serious issues of life.

Teens cannot know exactly how the details of discipleship will work for them (and neither can we). But what they must grasp and have the maturity to understand is the basic parameters of the decisions they are making. Then, when specific challenges arise, they will be more prepared and prayerfully will remain faithful.

Motivation

Motivations for any of us can become confused and clouded. The Bible teaches that our hearts are deceitful (Jeremiah 17:9) and that we cannot always accurately judge our own selves (1 Corinthians 4:3-4). If this is difficult for adults, how much more difficult will it be for inexperienced and unseasoned youth.

Here are some unworthy motivations that can creep into a young person's heart as they consider making a decision to follow Jesus:

- A desire to please their parents
- A hunger to be accepted in the church teen group
- To do "expected" thing at a certain age
- A superficial quest to be rid of a guilty conscience
- To avoid going to hell—a fire insurance policy

We can see that these motives all have some basis of truth in them but that they fall short of what the Lord requires of true disciples. Here are some of the motives Jesus wants:

- Love for God above any other love in life
- Sincere faith in God and in Jesus Christ as his Son
- Deep convictions about God's word
- Appreciation for, and dependence upon, God's grace
- A personal response to the cross of Christ
- A passionate desire to follow, serve and imitate Jesus
- A sincere awareness of the need for forgiveness of sin
- A realization of separation from God apart from Christ
- A determination to make a difference for God in the world

We must help our kids sort through their motivations. Some teens have an accurate picture of themselves and have hearts that are easily understood and purely motivated. Other teens are more complicated and need help to sort themselves out.

Some kids may be oblivious to the fact that their motives are not deep enough or are wrongly based. If so, then we must use the Scriptures to guide them to self-awareness. In doing this, let me caution you against making young people become so introspective that they begin to completely doubt themselves. We can get them so knotted up inside that they don't know which end is up.

Other kids are more hard-hearted and calloused. They can take, and will need, stronger challenges to their sincerity. Don't be naive. If we fail to see through their masks and deceptions, they may never come to grips with their sin and be truly converted.

Above all, pray for wisdom and seek advice. As parents we need help in being objective on these touchy, difficult judgment calls.

Method

How do we proceed? Who should be involved in helping our children become disciples? What is our role in the process? How much should we be involved? Precise answers to these questions elude us because there are simply too many variables involved:

First, the status of our current relationship with our kids—is it close or strained?

Second, do our children find it easy or difficult to be open with us?

Third, what is the level of our own experience, wisdom and insight in working with people in general?

Fourth, are there any family conflicts that will have to be worked through during our children's conversion process, and might we need outside help to resolve them?

These are just a few of the factors that need to be considered as our children near the time of their study to become disciples.

The best approach is to look at our children's conversion as a team effort. Our parental insight and influence is absolutely essential. We ought not take a passive, detached role. But the involvement of others is critical also. As parents we may not be objective in assessing our children's spiritual condition. We may be too hard or too soft, overly suspicious or completely naive. Involving other people assures that our children get the benefit of the best counsel and help we can provide them during this all-important time.

The other key people are our kids' friends who are already disciples. Having someone their own age to open up with makes a big difference. As peers, these young friends can better understand our kids' feelings, needs and struggles. They also serve as role models. Nothing replaces these fellow teens who serve as "best friends" and as living proof that it can be done.

I remember watching my daughter Elizabeth play this crucial role in the lives of one of her friends, a girl she helped lead to Christ when we lived in New Jersey. This young teenager was studying the Bible with some of the women in the church. Elizabeth got involved in the studies, and over time they became close friends. I still remember all the many talks they had as

Elizabeth's friend worked through all that she was being taught. Elizabeth was able to share, as a peer, what she went through and the questions she had to answer in her own coming to Christ. It made a great difference. Her friend was indeed baptized into Christ, and now, many years later, they are still close friends.

Means of understanding

In bringing our kids to conviction about their sins, we must employ great wisdom. I urge the careful study of Luke 15:11–31, commonly known as the parable of the prodigal son. This simple story of Jesus is brilliant in its grasp of human nature and will prove invaluable to us as we seek to understand the differences in our children.

Presented in the parable are the stories of two sons, a younger one who left home and an older one who remained with his father. The younger son was self-assertive and independent and outwardly rebelled against his father's will. He left home to indulge himself in the wild life of wine, women and song.

The older brother, while never openly defying his father's authority, had his own set of very serious problems. He was unhappy, unforgiving, ungrateful and resentful of his duties. He seethed with underlying anger and felt mistreated and short-changed by his father. Although he lived in close proximity to his dad, he was far from him in heart and character.

What kinds of kids do we have living in our homes? I am sure that we can see in these two boys a reflection of the different attitudes of our own children.

Paul recognizes there are different kinds of sin and different kinds of sinners:

> The sins of some men are obvious, reaching the place of judgment ahead of them; the sins of others trail behind them. (1 Timothy 5:24)

263

We cannot be permissive with our rebellious, arrogant "younger brother" children, whose sins, in the language of Paul, are "obvious." They are so stubborn that the only way they can learn is to come to the end of their rope. If we bail them out of all of their "pigpens," we short-circuit the humbling process that brings them to their senses.

Our "older brother" kids require a different approach. Their sins "trail behind them" and are more subtle and difficult to recognize. If we try to treat them as if they are sexually loose or on the verge of becoming drug dealers, we are making a very serious mistake. It only frustrates kids like this when they feel they must uncover some dramatic sin in order to be converted.

But we and they must realize that their sins are just as serious as those of the rebellious younger brother. In one sense, we even should be more wary here, because the story concludes with a restored younger son but with a stubborn, impenitent older son arguing with his father on the back steps.

In the case of my daughter Elizabeth, she became sidetracked during her conversion process in just the manner I am describing. She studied Galatians 5:19–21 and vainly searched her life for sins like sexual immorality, drunkenness, etc. What she failed to see was that her sins were primarily those of attitude—sins like pride, independence and envy. She became so frustrated and confused that she actually gave up trying for a period of time.

Several months later, she began to seek a relationship with God once again. I had a heart-to-heart talk with Elizabeth in which I helped her see that her greatest problems were her pride, self-sufficiency and independence in her relationship with God and with other people. We talked about a telling remark she made to her mother on one occasion, "Maybe I can have a good life and accomplish great things without God."

After seeing what her real issues were, Elizabeth was humbled and sobered. She grieved over the way she had treated God after all that he had given to her. She repented and was baptized into Christ shortly afterwards.

Many prayers

What better way to close our thoughts on conversion than this? We should pray for our children daily. Beyond all of the wisdom, expertise, methods and words, God must move in their hearts and lives. Before my children were born (or conceived), I prayed that they would one day give their lives to Jesus. I still pray for them now, and I will continue to do so until I die. Their names will always be held up in my prayers before the throne of God wherever they are and whatever their spiritual condition.

Prayer is the greatest work we can do on our children's behalf. Ultimately, only God himself can reach our children. We have a role to play, but it is not the leading role. We are to point our kids to One greater than ourselves. He has the ability to win their hearts and inspire their faith, and he will be at work throughout their lives to help them find their way to their soul's true home.

Epilogue

It is our desire that this book lighten your load, not make it heavier. In that spirit we want to help you know how to respond, and how not to respond, to what we have taught.

We leave you with some pointers that can help you get started and stay on track.

Begin where you are. It is not too late to start. Even if your children are older, you can still make a big difference in their lives. Do not be discouraged because you have made mistakes, even of the worst sort. Do not waste time wishing you could do it all over. Courageously face your failures, learn from them, and move forward to better things. The God we serve is a God of forgiveness and recovery.

Start with the basics. Chapter 1 ("First Things First") and chapter 9 ("Foundations of a Spiritual Family") form the platform upon which the rest of the teaching of this book is built. Begin there, and add the rest as you gain spiritual strength.

Get help. There is no way a book can replace the tailor-made advice of wise, spiritual people. God has given us the church to encourage us and to provide real-world guidance. Life is too complicated for theoretical answers—we need hands-on help.

Do not give up. In trying to implement the principles and teachings in this book, you may find that you and your family members do not change as quickly or as completely as you would like. Nowhere are weaknesses more exposed than in family relationships. You did not get where you are overnight, and the changes you are striving to make will take time. Keep a high ideal, but measure progress by how far you have come from your starting point.

Allow God to move and work. God is arranging the events of your life to train and discipline you and your family. Given time, he can turn even the greatest of difficulties into a blessing. Work, but pray, and wait on God to do what only he can do.

"Don't be afraid.... Remember the Lord, who is great and awesome, and fight for your brothers, your sons and your daughters, your wives and your homes." (Nehemiah 4:14)

Recommended Reading

Family Devotionals

Ziegler, Tom and Lori. *As for Me and My House: 50 Easy-to-Use Devotionals for Families—Volume 1*. Spring Hill, TN: DPI, 1999.

Ziegler, Tom and Lori. *As for Me and My House: 50 Easy-to-Use Devotionals Preteens and Young Teens—Volume 2*. Spring Hill, TN: DPI, 2008.

Schmitt, Lois, Ed. *Scriptures to Grow On: A Family Handbook*. Spring Hill, TN: DPI, 2001.

Scott, John, and Kim Scott. *One Picture's Worth: Memorizing God's Words*. Spring Hill, TN: DPI, 2008.

Sex Education

Girard, Linda, and Rodney Pate. *My Body Is Private*. Morton Grove, IL: Albert Whitman & Company, 1992.

Jance, Judith. *It's Not Your Fault*. Charlotte, NC: Kidsrights, 1985.

Mayo, Mary Ann. *God's Good Gift: Teaching Your Kids About Sex (Ages 8–11)*. Grand Rapids: Zondervan, 1991.

General Parenting

Chapman, Gary, and Ross Campbell. *The Five Love Languages of Children*. Chicago: Northfield Publishing, 1997.

Jacoby, Douglas and Vickie. *The Quiver: Christian Parenting in a Non-Christian World*. Spring, TX: Illumination Publishers International, 2005.

Laing, Sam, and Geri Laing and Elizabeth Laing Thompson. *The Wonder Years: Parenting Preteens and Teens*. Spring Hill, TN: DPI, 2001.

Rosemond, John. *Ending the Homework Hassle*. Riverside, NJ: Andrews McMeel Publishing, 1990.

Thompson, Elizabeth Laing. *Glory Days: Real Life Answers for Teens*. Spring Hill, TN: DPI, 1999.

Marriage

Baird, Gloria, and Kay McKean. *Love Your Husband*. Spring Hill, TN: DPI, 2001.

Hendricks, William, and Robert Lewis. *Rocking the Roles: Building a Win-Win Marriage*. Colorado Springs: NavPress, 1999.

Laing, Sam, and Geri Laing. *Friends and Lovers: Marriage As God Designed It*. Spring Hill, TN: DPI, 1996.

Laing, Sam. *The Five Senses of Romantic Love: God's Plan for Exciting Sexual Intimacy in Marriage*. Spring Hill, TN: DPI, 2008.

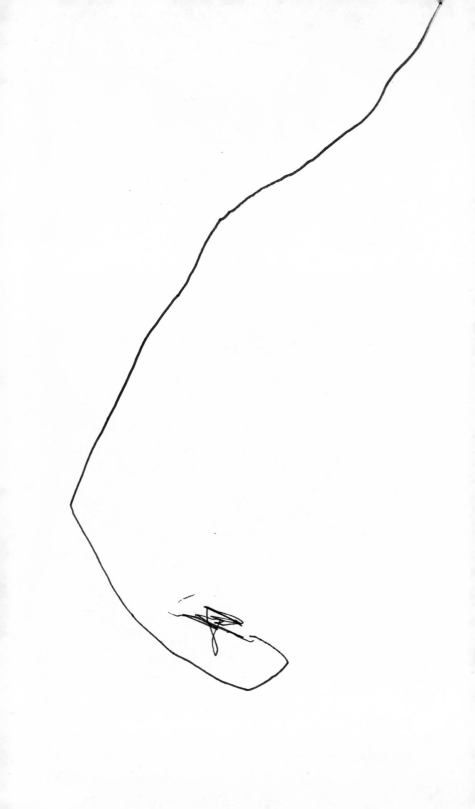